W. H. Davenport (William Henry Davenport) Adams

Famous caves and catacombs : described and illustrated

W. H. Davenport (William Henry Davenport) Adams

Famous caves and catacombs : described and illustrated

ISBN/EAN: 9783743606395

Printed in Europe, USA, Canada, Australia, Japan

Cover: Foto ©ninafisch / pixelio.de

Manufactured and distributed by brebook publishing software (www.brebook.com)

W. H. Davenport (William Henry Davenport) Adams

Famous caves and catacombs : described and illustrated

FIGURE OF A GRAVE-DIGGER, CATACOMB OF ST. CALIXTUS, ROME.

Page 123.

THOMAS NELSON AND SONS,
London, Edinburgh, and New York.

ᶠAMOUS CAVES

AND

CATACOMBS

𝔇escribed and 𝔍llustrated.

By

W. H. DAVENPORT ADAMS.

WITH 40 ILLUSTRATIONS.

𝔏ondon:

T. NELSON AND SONS, PATERNOSTER ROW.

EDINBURGH; AND NEW YORK.

1888.

Preface.

THE following pages contain an account of the most
famous Caves and Cave-temples in the world, in which
the researches of modern antiquaries have discovered
the remains of a prehistoric age. In order to give com-
pleteness to the view of the subject, brief sketches have
been added of the Catacombs of Rome and of Paris.
It may be objected that these are artificial rather than
natural excavations; but they have an obvious connection with the general subject, both in their present
character and in the uses to which they have been
applied.

Every one will be ready to admit the importance of
giving to the study of Nature in all its aspects a prominent place in the education of the young. There is
now no lack of text-books devoted to this subject; but
they are generally restricted in their scope, and from
their very comprehensiveness they are meagre in their
details.

The present volume and its companions have been
compiled as supplementary to more precise and metho-
dical treatises. It is their aim to treat with some ful-
ness the natural objects described in them,—to deal

with them in a familiar and entertaining manner, with copious supply of anecdote, narrative, and illustration. Scientific accuracy has been aimed at in the statement of principles, and in setting forth the results of modern research; but the main object has been to collect all such descriptive and entertaining matter bearing on the subjects discussed as would impress the youthful mind with the interest and importance of these studies.

The present volume is peculiarly interesting from its subject, taking the reader to the border lands of natural history and archæology, as well as to those of paganism and Christianity. As it contains a mass of valuable details not easily accessible to the reader elsewhere, we venture to claim for it a favourable reception at the hands of the public.

Contents.

V.—Modern Times.

List of Illustrations.

FAMOUS CAVES AND CATACOMBS.

I.

Ancient Egypt.

THE GREAT CAVE-TEMPLE OF IPSAMBUL.

IN his ascent of that part of the course of the Nile which is included within the boundaries of Lower Nubia, at a distance of sixty leagues south-west of the First Cataract, and twelve leagues north of the Last, the traveller, who has been painfully impressed by the poor and desolated aspect of the country, pauses suddenly, struck with astonishment and admiration, before a range of colossal statues carved out of the rocky side of a hill of limestone, named *Djebel Abou-Simbel*, the base of which is washed by the waters of the famous river.

For centuries the shifting sands of the Desert had accumulated over the architectural wonders of Abou-Simbel, or Ipsambul, and no sign of them was visible but the head of one gigantic statue.

No traveller seems to have inquired what this solitary landmark *meant;* whether it indicated the site of a city, a palace, or a tomb; until, in 1717, the enthusiastic Belzoni, accompanied by Captains Irby and Mangles, undertook the work of excavation. Their toil was well rewarded; for it brought to light a magnificent specimen of the highest Egyptian art; a specimen which, with Champollion, we may confidently attribute to the palmiest epoch of Pharaonic civilization.

Every voyager who visits Ipsambul seems inspired with more than ordinary feelings of admiration.

Here, exclaims Eliot Warburton, the daring genius of Ethiopian architecture ventured to enter into rivalry with Nature's greatness, and found her material in the very mountains that seemed to bid defiance to her efforts.*

You can conceive nothing more singular and impressive, says Mrs. Romer,† than the façade of the Great Temple; for it is both a temple and a cave. Ipsambul, remarks Sir F. Henniker, ‡ is the *ne plus ultra* of Egyptian labour; and in itself an ample recompense for the labour of a voyage up the Nile. There is no temple, of either Dendera, Thebes, or Philae, which can be put in competition with it; and one may well be contented to finish one's travels with having seen the noblest monument of antiquity in Nubia and Egypt.

There are two temples at Ipsambul—one much larger than the other; but each has a *speos,* or cavern, hewn out of the solid rock. Let us first visit the more considerable, consecrated by Rameses II. to the sun-god Phrah, or

* Eliot Warburton, "The Crescent and the Cross," i., c. xiii.
† Mrs. Romer, "Temples and Tombs of Egypt and Nubia," i. 207.
‡ Sir F. Henniker, "Notes during a Visit to Egypt," p. 100.

siris, whose statue is placed above the entrance-door-
ay.

An area of about 187 feet wide by 86 feet high is
cavated from the mountain, the sides being perfectly
mooth, except where ornamented by relievos. The
çade consists of four colossal statues of Rameses II.
ated, and each about 65 feet high ; two being placed on
ther side of a narrow gate. From the shoulder to the
ira they measure 15 feet 6 inches ; the ears, 3 feet 6
ches ; the face, 7 feet ; the beard, 5 feet 6 inches ; across

FACADE OF THE TEMPLE OF PHRAH—IPSAMBUL.

e shoulders, 25 feet 4 inches. The moulding of each
ony countenance is exquisite. The beauty of the curves
surprising in the stone ; the rounding of the muscles,
d the flowing lines of the neck and face, are executed
th great fidelity.

Connoisseurs seem never weary of expatiating upon the
rmonious proportions of these colossal visages, which
e the more surprising as the artist could have been
ided by no model.

Between the legs of these gigantic Ramessids are placed

four statues of greatly inferior dimensions ; mere pigmies compared with their colossal neighbours, and yet considerably larger than ordinary human size.

The doorway is about twenty feet high. We have already referred to the statue of the sun-god which surmounts it. On either side are carved some huge hieroglyphical bas-reliefs; while the whole façade is finished by a cornice and row of quaintly carved figures underneath a frieze of monkeys, one-and twenty in number and each measuring eight feet in height and six feet across the shoulders.

SITTING FIGURE OF RAMESES II.—IPSANBUL.

Passing through the doorway, you enter the *pronaos*, "a vast and gloomy hall, such as Eblis might have given Vathek audience in." Here, as soon as the eye grows accustomed to the prevailing twilight, it defines the proportions of a vast, mysterious aisle, so to speak, whose pillars are formed by eight colossal giants on whom the rays of heaven have never shone. They stand erect, with hands crossed on each stony breast figures of the all-conquering Rameses, whose mitre-shaped

l-dresses, each wearing in front the serpent, the em-
n of royal power, nearly touch the roof.   They are all
ectly alike; all carry the crosier and flagellum; every
 is characterized by a deep and solemn expression.
ilant, serene, benign, says Miss Martineau, here they
d; teaching us to inquire reverentially into the early
ers and conditions of that human mind which was

PRONAOS OF THE TEMPLE OF PHRAH—IPSAMBUL.

able of such conceptions of abstract qualities as are
esented in their forms.   How different from the
esque and often unclean monsters which embody the
du's ideas of Divine attributes !   These are the very
es of conscious power, of calm and passionless intellect;
ar removed from the petty things of earth as are the stars
eaven from "the worm that crawls beneath the sod."*

* Harriet Martineau, "Eastern Life," L 197.

These images of the great king are supported against
enormous pillars, cut out of the solid rock; and behind
them run two gorgeous galleries, whose walls are covered
with historical bas-reliefs of battle and victory, of con-
quering warriors, bleeding victims, fugitives, cities be-
sieged, long trains of soldiers and captives, numerous
companies of chariots, all combined in a picture of great
beauty and impressive effect.

The pronaos measures 57 feet by 52 feet.   It opens
into the *naos* or *cella*, which is only 37 feet broad, 25½
feet long, and 22 feet high.   It is supported in the centre
by four pillars, each about three feet square; and its walls
are also embellished with fine hieroglyphs in an excellent
state of preservation.

Next, through these different doors we may pass into
a still smaller chamber, the *sekos*, or sanctuary, 23 feet by
12 feet; where, upon thrones of rock, are seated the three
divinities of the *Trimourti* or Egyptian Trinity, Ammon-
Ra, Phrah, and Phtah, accompanied by Rameses the Great,
here admitted to an equality with them.

On the right side of the pronaos, as you enter, two
doors may be seen at a short distance from each other,
which lead into separate chambers: the first, 39 feet long
and 11½ feet wide; the other, 48½ feet by 13 feet 3 inches.
At the lateral corners of the entrance from the pronaos
into the cella are other doors, each conducting into a room
hewn out of the "live rock," but with no visible means
of ventilation, and each 22½ feet long by 10 feet broad.
These rooms open into others, which communicate with the
sekos, and are 43 feet by 11 feet.   The six are profusely
adorned with representations of offerings to the gods, of
lamps, vases, flasks, and piles of cake and fruit.   The lotus

painted in every stage of its growth ; and the boat is a
quently repeated symbol.   In one place we see it borne
oft by a procession of priests, as a shrine, upon poles of
lm-trunks lashed together.   These bas-reliefs seem to
ve been covered with a coat of stucco, which was after-
rds painted in rich and varied tints.   The ground-
lour of the ceiling is blue ; it is framed, so to speak, in
ricoloured border, ornamented with symbolic birds.
Well may Champollion exclaim,—" The Temple of
sambul is in itself worth a journey to Nubia !"*
And Lenormant,—" It is the most gigantic conception
er begotten by the genius of the Pharaohs !"†
As for its antiquity, some authorities pretend that it is
e primitive model of all Egyptian architecture ; but the
eroglyphical legends, and the subjects of the bas-reliefs,
ry clearly prove that the temple belongs to the Nine-
enth or Theban dynasty, whose third Pharaoh, Rameses
., reigned about 1327 B.C., and who, as Sesostris, figures
gely in Greek history.

THE SMALLER SPEOS OF IPSAMBUL.

The Little Temple of Ipsambul was dedicated to Athor,
  Isis, the Egyptian Venus, by Nofré-Afri, queen of
meses the Great.
Either side of the doorway is flanked by three statues,
irty-five feet in height, sculptured in bold relief on the
mpact mass of rock, and standing erect, with their arms
aced rigidly against their sides.   The central in each
ad represents Nofré-Afri, as Isis, with her placid face

Champollion, " Lettres écrites d'Egypte et de Nubie en 1828 ot 1829."
Lenormant, " Esquisse de la Basse Nubie" (*Revue Française*, Nov. 1839).

surmounted by the usual emblem, a moon contained within cow's horns. The other images are those of Rameses and his eldest son; or, as some writers assert, are both Ramessids. Beneath the right hand of each statue stands a smaller one, about seven feet high; the six figures being intended for the three sons and three daughters of the king and queen.

A portion of the rock measuring one hundred and eleven feet in length has been excavated to make room for the façade of the temple. The devices begin on the northern side with an image of Rameses brandishing his falchion, as if about to strike. Athor, behind him, lifts her hand in compassion for the victim; Osiris, in front, holds forth the great knife, as if to command the slaughter. He is seated there as the judge, and decides the fate of the peoples conquered by the Egyptian king. The next object is a colossal statue of about thirty feet high, wrought in a deep recess of the rock: it represents Athor standing, and two tall plumes spring from the middle of her head-dress, with the symbolic crescent on either side. Then comes a mass of hieroglyphics, and above them are seated the sun-god and the hawk-headed deity Anubis. On either side of the doorway, as you pass into the pronaos, offerings are presented to Athor,—who holds in her hand the lotus-headed sceptre, and is surrounded with a cloud of emblems and inscriptions. This hall is supported by six square pillars, all having the head of Athor on the front face of their capitals; the other three faces being occupied with sculptures, once richly painted, and still exhibiting traces of blue, red, and yellow colouring. The shafts are covered with hieroglyphs, and emblematical representations of Osiris, Athor, Kneph, and other deities.

Within the pronaos a transverse corridor ends in two
ide chambers; and beyond the corridor, or naos, lies the
kos, or sanctuary, where Athor is revealed in all her
ajesty, with the lunar crescent as a crown upon her head.

The total length of the speos, which stands only a few
irds from the river-bank, and about twenty feet above
s present level, is seventy-six feet. A number of ovals,
: *cartouches*, as Champollion calls them, containing the
ime and praenomen of Rameses II., are cut in several
laces of the square border that encloses the façade of the
imple, like a frame, and on the buttresses between the
ilossal figures.

It has been remarked that these edifices, even in their
resent desolation and decay, and encrusted as they are
ith the smoke from the fires of the wandering Kennous,
roduce a strange feeling of awe in the mind of the spec-
itor. But what must have been their effect when the
irine contained its mystic images; when the open portals
ivealed the glorious perspective of columns freshly sculp-
ired, and walls glowing in new colours, to the wondering
nd worshipping multitude, as far back as the sekos itself;
hen the roof shone with azure and gold, like a starry
cy; when the colossal forms planted in silent majesty
n their stony pedestals represented to all who gazed the
eities in whom they reposed their faith; when along the
irch-lit aisles passed the long procession of king, and
obles, and priests in gorgeous robes; when the adytum
as filled with clouds of sweet incense, and the vaults
isounded with the surging music of tens of thousands
f voices; when every hieroglyph and emblem, now so
leaningless, conveyed some significant idea to the kneel-
ig votary?

THE OTHER SPEOS, OR CAVE-TEMPLES, OF NUBIA.

The two speos of Ipsambul are not the only ones we meet with in Nubia.   Numerous others bear witness to the wonderful patience of the ancient Egyptian population, and to the power and force of the religious sentiment by which they were animated.   They are well worth a visit, though inferior both in beauty and magnificence to the two speos we have just described.   Moreover, they are constructed on the same plan, and seem to belong to the same epoch.

Among the most remarkable we may refer to that of *Derr*, or *Derri*, which, like the larger temple at Ipsambul, was constructed by, or in honour of, Rameses II.   It was dedicated to Ammon-Ra, the supreme god, and Phrah, the sun-god.   The pronaos is fronted with four colossal Osiride figures.   The only part of the temple excavated out of the rock is the sekos, the roof of which is supported by six square columns.   The walls are sculptured in what has been termed *relieved intaglios ;* that is, the outlines are cut in a groove, the depth of which affords the necessary relief to the interior.

The entire depth in the rock is one hundred and ten feet.

At *Ibrim*, the *Princis Magna* of the Romans,* there are four rock-temples ; all of different epochs, but all belonging to the Pharaonic age.

The most ancient dates back as far as the reign of Thothmosis I., or about 1500 B.C.   Four figures, about one-third larger than nature, are seated in the furthest

Kenrick, " Ancient Egypt." II. 464.

ecess : the two central represent the royal founder ; the
others, the patron-deity of Ibrim, the hawk-headed Thoth,
and the goddess Sata, the Egyptian Juno, the divinity of
Elephantina and Nubia.

The second speos belongs to the reign of Thothmosis
II., or Moeris, whose statue is placed in a niche in the
sekos, between the images of Thoth and Sata. An inscription above the entrance records that this speos was
constructed by a prince named Nahi, governor of Nubia.

The third dates from the reign of Amenophis II., successor of Thothmosis III.

The fourth is less ancient, belonging to the epoch of
Rameses the Great. It was constructed by a governor of
Nubia in honour of the patron-gods of Ibrim, the hawk-
headed Thoth and Sata, and to the glory of the Pharaoh,
whose statue is seated, in the sekos, between those of the
two divinities.

The traveller may also visit in the neighbourhood of
Tosco, surrounded by a remarkable landscape, a subterranean monument somewhat rudely excavated in the
rock, which seems to have been used as a place of sepulture rather than as a temple. Burckhardt speaks of another and not dissimilar subterranean vault, about one
hour's journey from the Nile.

In the same quarter, and on the bank of the river,
near the island of Kette, may be seen the entrances of a
certain number of tombs hollowed out of the rock up to
a height of thirty-nine to forty-eight feet.

And, lastly, at Kalabshé, where

"Desolation keeps unbroken Sabbath,
'Mid caves and temples, palaces and sepulchres,"

may be seen two remarkable temples, one of which is a

speos. Harriet Martineau describes the latter as full of the glory of the great Rameses. It is dedicated to Ammon-Ra, the "Unknown and Unutterable, the God of Gods;" Kneph, or Knuph, the ram-headed god, in conjunction with Phtah; and the virgin goddess of purity, Anouké.*

We approach the entrance of the cavern between quarried rocks, carved with curious sculpture. On one side sits Rameses enthroned, receiving the costly tribute and servile homage of the conquered Ethiopians, among whom may be recognized—for they are named—the Prince of Cush and his two children. You may see, too, oxen and gazelles, lions and antelopes, camelopards, apes, elephants' teeth, quaint gorgeous fans, bags of gold, and heaps of ostriches' eggs; Ethiopia has poured out all her wealth to bribe the victor's clemency. A few steps further, and you behold the battle-scene which was the prelude to this triumph. It glows with a rude but vigorous life: the foe is flying; a wounded chief is carried on the shoulders of his warriors; Rameses, sweeping by in his chariot, bends his mighty bow; a peasant-boy, flinging dust upon his head, laments the downfall of his country.

Turn to the other side, and your eye rests upon additional pictures of "the storm and strife;" all designed for the glorification of the great sovereign who erected this temple as a sign of thanksgiving for his victories and a monument to his fame.

The temple contains but two divisions; a pronaos, and a sekos. The walls, as usual, are everywhere blazoned with hieroglyphs and pictures. It is said that a Moslem hermit once made his abode here, and probably much of the fine Egyptian work was defaced by his iconoclastic hands.

* Martineau, "Eastern Life," i. 232.

THE HEMI-SPEOS OF NUBIA.

In addition to the speos, or temples completely subterranean in construction, Egypt and Nubia contain several
temples of which a part only is excavated in the rock, the
other part being constructed with hewn stones. These
are called *hemi-speos.*

Of all the Nubian hemi-speos, I suppose the most interesting is that of *Ghirsché-Housseyn ;* a small village
situated on the left bank of the Nile, in Lower Nubia,
and on the very site of an ancient town, named *Phthaheï*
or *Thypthah* * (the Roman *Tutzis*).

The most ancient section of this hemi-speos, which was,
at the same time, the most necessary for the Egyptian
cultus, is excavated in a limestone rock, rising like a
precipitous cliff above the level of the yellow sandy desert.
The more modern portion, comprising the *area* and
propyla, is built of sandstone, and greatly dilapidated.
Four pillars alone are standing, which formerly connected
the colonnade of the propyla with the speos properly so
called. These four pillars are ornamented with colossal
statues, wearing the *pschent* or tiara-shaped head-dress,
and carrying in their hands, which are folded across their
breasts, the flail and crosier, the usual emblems of Osiris.

The *speos* properly so called is divided, like the speos
we have already described, into *pronaos, naos,* and *sekos.*

The pronaos is a vast hall supported by six enormous pillars, in each of which has been hollowed out
a effigy, twenty feet in height. Each of the eight
square niches in the side-walls encloses a group of three

---

* Sir Gardner Wilkinson, "Manners and Customs of the Ancient Egyptians,"
. 250.

deities,—Phtah, his companion Athor, and Rameses in
the centre.

"Accustomed as I had been," says Burckhardt,* "to the
grandeur of Egyptian temples, I was, nevertheless, struck
with admiration on entering this gloomy pronaos, and be-
holding these immense figures standing in triumph before
me." After describing the lateral recesses and their sculptured groups, he adds: "All these, as well as the colossi, are
covered with a thick coat of stucco, and had once been
painted; they must then have worn a splendid appearance. A door leads from the pronaos into the cella, in the
middle of which are two massy pillars, and on either side
a small apartment, which was probably a place of sepulture: on the floor of each are high stone benches, which
may have served for supporting mummies, or perhaps as
tables for embalming the bodies deposited in the temple."

In the sekos are four seated figures, much larger than
the natural size, which seem to represent Phrah, Rameses,
Phtah, and Athor.

The whole length of the speos is one hundred and thirty
feet in the rock. It is specially remarkable for the severity
of its style and the imposing aspect of its architecture. The
impression which it produces is considerably enhanced
by the circumstance that the temple receives no other
light than that afforded by the entrance-doorway.

In its aspect we recognize a certain primitiveness, says
Gailhabaud, which recalls the sombre majesty of the past;
an undefinable something which saddens the heart while
elevating the thought. We are seized with astonishment
on entering this mysterious speos, and contemplating its
heavy colossal figures.

* Burckhardt, "Travels in Nubia," pp. 99, 100.

From the beautiful execution of the bas-reliefs, com-
red with the ruder sculpture of the colossal statues
ich, at the entrance of the speos, stand out so promi-
ntly, and impress the imagination by their imposing
oportions, but which, when viewed near at hand, ap-
ar little better than shapeless masses, several authori-
s have concluded that the temple of Ghirsché-Housseyn
longs to the very infancy of the Pharaonic architecture,
t that it was restored and adorned with bas-reliefs by
imeses the Great.

HYPOGEA OF BENI-HASSAN EL GADIM.

" Monarchs, the powerful and the strong,
Famous in history and in song
Of olden time."—LONGFELLOW.

The rock-tombs, or hypogea, of Beni-Hassan are. with
ɔ exception of the Pyramids, the oldest known monu-
ints in Egypt, and it is probable that many of them
ceived their tenants long before Joseph ruled as viceroy
the Egyptian king. They are situated in a hollow of
ɔ hills up above the village of Beni-Hassan, and it is
possible to visit them without profit.
One tomb is of quite peculiar interest. It dates from
ɔ reign of Osirtesen I., and may be described, in few
ırds, as an arched cavern, whose walls are everywhere
ıminated with the speaking signs of a pictorial lan-
age. The entrance is in a vaulted portico, which rests
two shapely pillars not unlike the Doric in character.
roughout its chambers the basement is painted a deep
l; and on this red the hieroglyphics are "picked out"
green. The central aisle has a low covered roof, and
its extremity a large niche or recess. It is divided

from the lateral aisles by a range of columns, resembling those of the portico.

A remarkable procession forms the subject of one of the pictures in this "painted chamber." Some authorities have erroneously supposed it to represent the arrival of Joseph's brethren in Egypt; but not only is it of older date, its groups and devices prove that it has no connection with any event in Hebrew history.

EXTERIOR OF ROCK-TOMB—BENI-HASSAN.

At either end of the long train of figures stands one who is evidently a great official, and whom we learn to have been named Nefothph, the governor of the district, and, probably, the owner of the tomb. To him, as the old play-books say, enters a dreary train of seven-and-thirty captives; captives with white complexions, tunics, sandals, and long beards; the women with dishevelled hair, and

ıod in ankle-boots. They bring with them offerings to
ppease the great man's anger,—a wild goat, a gazelle, a
ɔck of ostriches, and an ibis.

In other and less important tombs we meet with the
ɹd Egyptian symbols, the lotus and the papyrus. Some
ᴀve slightly vaulted roofs, and some are furnished with
ᴜaller inner chambers; while all are astir, so to speak,
ith the ancient life,—with the manners and customs,

INTERIOR OF ROCK-TOMB—BENI-HASSAN.

ᴛe occupations and pastimes, of a generation who
ᴏurished four or five thousand years ago. Nowhere
lse in the world can be found so curious a history of a
eople, written or painted by themselves.

We have here, says Miss Martineau,* of whose animated
escription we shall freely avail ourselves, the art of writ-

* Martineau, " Eastern Life," II. 35—41.

ing as a familiar practice, in the scribes who are numbering the stones on every hand. There are ships which
would look handsome in Southampton Water any sunny
day. There are glass-blowers who might be from New-
castle, but for their dress and complexion. There are
flax-dressers, spinners, weavers, and a production of cloth
which an English manufacturer would study with interest.
There are potters, painters, carpenters, and statuaries.
There is a doctor attending a patient, and a herdsman
physicking cattle. The hunters employ arrows, spears,
and the lasso. The lasso is as evident as on the Pampas
at this day. There is the Nile full of fish, and a hip-
popotamus among the ooze. There is the bastinado for
the men; and the flogging of a seated woman. Nothing
is more extraordinary than the gymnastics and other
games of the women. Their various games of ball are
excellent. The great men are attended by dwarfs and
buffoons, as in a much later age; and it is clear that
bodily infirmity was treated with contempt,—deformed
and decrepit personages appearing in the discharge of the
meanest offices. It was an age when this might be looked
for; and when war would be the most prominent occupa-
tion, and wrestling the prevailing sport, and probably also
the discipline of the soldiery; and when hunting, fishing,
and fowling would be very important pursuits. But,
then, how remarkable a power of representing these
things is here! And what luxury coexisting with these
early pursuits! Here are harpers with their harps of
seven strings; and garments and boat-sails with elegant
patterns and borders, where, by the way, angular and
regular figures are pointedly preferred; and the ladies'
hair, disordered and flying about in their sports, has tails

tassels, very like what may have been seen in London
wing-rooms in no very remote times. The incident
ch most clearly reminds one of the antiquity of these
itings is, that the name of bird, beast, fish, or artificer,
ritten up over the object delineated. It is the re-
rce—not needed here, however—of the artist who
te on his picture, "This is the man," "This is the

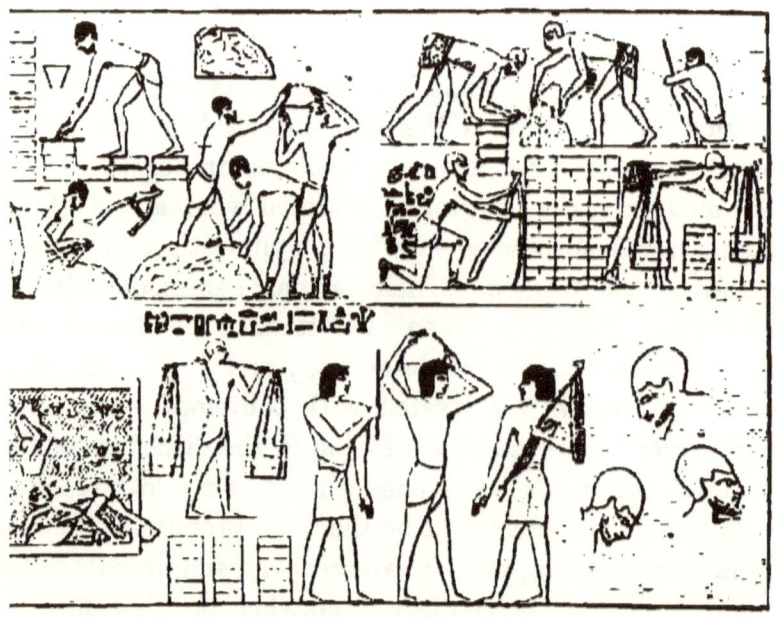

BRICKMAKERS.
(From the Tombs of Beni-Hassan.)

ikey." Another barbarism is, that the great man, the
ipant of the tomb, has his greatness signified by big-
s, being a giant among middle-sized people. There
brickmakers also, who are shown going through the
erent processes of their craft; and they are supposed
some writers (but without foundation for the supposi-
i) to be the Jews in bondage.

THE GROTTOES OF SAMOUN, OR CAVES OF THE CROCODILES.

The famous Grottoes of Samoun, or Caves of the Crocodiles, are immense subterranean excavations, situated in Upper Egypt, not far from Monfalout.   They are filled with a truly incalculable quantity of human mummies, and mummies of quadrupeds, birds, and reptiles ; especially of those of crocodiles,—whence comes the popular designation by which these caves are known.   It is supposed that this mummy population came from the ancient city which occupied the site of Monfalout, and from the great Hermenopolis,—both situated on the left bank of the Nile.

The Grottoes of Samoun have not been very frequently explored; either because travellers generally do not know of their existence, or because those who have attempted the enterprise have been repelled at the outset by its difficulty and gloominess. A contemporary traveller, however,—M. A. Georges,*—informs us that he noticed on their black walls, near the mummy-heap, the name of a Roman lady, carefully engraved, and in large characters, among some other names.   But, even in the country to which they belong, these grottoes inspire the people with a superstitious terror, and it is not always easy to procure a guide who will lead you into their dreary recesses.

The entrance is a simple cranny or fissure level with the ground, and measuring about three feet three inches in diameter by nearly ten feet in depth.   After gliding or insinuating yourself through this air-hole, you crawl, rather than walk, along a narrow winding corridor, whose bottom is a fine and very soft sand, rising under your

* "Excursion aux Grottes de Samoun" (*Tour du Monde*, 1862, 1ᵉʳ Semestre).

ootsteps in an impalpable dust which renders respiration
ifficult. The obscurity is complete, and you have only
he pale gleam of the tapers to direct you in your painful
ourney.

After a considerable interval, says M. A. Georges, we
uit the sandy soil for a broken one, interrupted by great
ransversal stones. The sides of the tunnel contract,
nlarge, rise, sink, modulate, and often assume the form
f horizontal stalactites, menacing the head and breast
ike spears. Often you may partly stand upright, but
ften also you are compelled by sharp conical stones pen-
lent from the roof to bend almost to your knees. Occa-
ionally you come to a wider and loftier space, where you
an regain your full height, and walk erect; at such a
elief from your previous torture you rejoice as at an
asis in the desert. Finally you arrive at an enclosure of
ome extent, formed by a foundation of great stones piled
ıp one against another; here you advance as best you
an, creeping around or over it.

Some years ago, says M. A. Georges, the guides disco-
ered in this enclosure the corpse of a traveller who had
;one astray in the grottoes, and had come to this spot
o die of famine and exhaustion. M. Maxime du Camp
urnishes an impressive description of this corpse in his
' Narrative of Travel in Egypt and Nubia."

On raising their eyes, he says, he and his companions
erceived a horrible spectacle. A corpse, still covered
vith its skin, was seated on a rounded fragment of rock;
ts aspect was hideous. It stretched out its arms like a
nan who yawns when he awakes; his head, thrown back,
ınd convulsed by agony, had bent his thin and withered
ıeck. His emaciated body, his eyes disproportionably

large, his chin contracted by a superhuman effort, his mouth twisted and wide open, as if for a last sad cry, his hair erect upon his head, all his features distorted by frightful suffering, gave him a horrible appearance. It made one shudder; involuntarily one thought of one's-self. His shrunken hands dug their nails into the flesh; the chest was split open, displaying the lungs and tracheal artery; on striking the abdomen, it resounded hoarsely, like a cracked drum.

Undoubtedly this man had been full of vital force when seized by death. Undoubtedly he had lost himself in these dark galleries, and his lantern having flickered out, he had vainly sought the track leading to the upper air, shouting in frenzied tones which none could hear; hunger, thirst, fatigue, terror, must have driven him nearly mad; he had seated himself on this stone, and howled despairingly until death had mercifully come to his relief. The warm humidity and the bituminous exhalations of the cavern had so thoroughly interpenetrated his body, that now his skin was black, tanned, imperishable, like that of a mummy. It was eight years since the poor wretch had been lost.

On quitting this spot of mournful memory, they turned to the left through a corridor whose roof and walls were blackened by bituminous vapours, and in which it was possible to walk upright. Thousands of bats, attracted by the travellers' torches, assailed them with a whirr of wings, and considerably impeded their progress. They then arrived at the most interesting part of the grottoes : the soil, which gave way beneath their feet, was composed of the débris of mummies and their swathings; at every step arose a black, acrid, nauseating dust, as bitter

s a compound of soot and aloes. An enormous number
f crocodiles of all sizes encumber the galleries; some are
lack, some corpulent, some gigantic, others not larger
han lizards. Side by side with the crocodiles they saw
nnumerable mummies of every kind, human mum-
ies and mummies of animals, placed close together

INTERIOR OF THE GROTTOES OF SAMOUN.

nd one upon each other in strata, so to speak, separated
nly by layers of palm leaves in remarkable preserva-
ion. The human mummies, carefully surrounded by
andages, were generally compressed between two boards

of sycamore, a wood reputed to be as incorruptible as
cedar.

Thus did they press forward along this road paved
with dead bodies, a road constantly extending before
them, sombre and profound; and God knows where they
would have terminated but for the fatigue, the oppression,
the want of light, the eager desire to return to the fresh
air of day, ill at ease as they were, and weary of funereal
impressions. They found the heat almost insupportable.
By trampling amongst the shreds and refuse, moreover,
they raised a dust which constantly grew thicker, and
penetrated, like a caustic, into eyes and nose and mouth,
and, so to speak, into every pore.

It seems that one day a fire broke out in these grottoes,
either through the imprudence of an Englishman or an
American, or, as some say, of a party of Arabs who had
entered them in search of bats, an excellent manure, and
carried their lamps of oil with the wicks in them all exposed. The conflagration spread into every gallery, and
lasted, according to one account, for three years; according to another, for a twelvemonth. However, it has not
left any very important traces behind it, perhaps because
the combustion, concentrated in such narrow and ill-
ventilated passages, took place very slowly.

THE CAVES OF THE LOWER THEBAID.

The Thebaid, or Upper Egypt, comprehending the deserts beyond the Libyan and Arabian chains of mountains, succeeded the Heptanomis, or Middle Egypt,
which terminated in the vicinity of Cuses,—that is to
say, nearly at the point where the Eastern Desert abuts

upon the Red Sea, in the same latitude as the extremity of the Sinaitic peninsula. The deserts of the South-East and the North-West furnished asylums for the Christian hermits who, inspired by their own erroneous interpretations of the prophecies of the evangelists Luke and Mark, imitated the example of St. Antony, and abandoned the world, to wait, with prayer and fasting, for the coming of their Lord.

It was about the end of the fourth century that it became generally known that the mountains and deserts of Egypt were full of these mistaken enthusiasts. Wonderful stories were told of their courage, their abstinence, their virtues, their miracles. Wonderful stories were told of their humility and charity : how that they called each other brothers ; and how that they behaved, each to each, with a love like that of David for Jonathan. How, too, they had all things in common, like the members of the Apostolic Church ; how they lived in peace and tranquillity, under a mild impartial rule ; and kept to the letter those injunctions of our Lord which the rest of the world had tacitly agreed to put aside.

The news spread. It chimed in, says Canon Kingsley,* with all that was best, as well as with much that was questionable, in the public mind at that epoch. " That men could be brothers ; that they could live without the tawdry luxury, the tasteless and often brutal amusements, the low sensuality, the base intrigues, the bloody warfare, which was the accepted lot of the many ; that they could find time to look steadfastly at heaven and hell as awful realities, which must be faced some day, which had best be faced at once,—this, just as much

* Canon Kingsley, " The Hermits," pp. 9-11.

as curiosity about their alleged miracles, and the selfish
longing to rival them in superhuman powers, led many of
the most virtuous and the most learned men of the time
to visit them and ascertain the truth.   Jerome, Rufinus,
Evagrius, Sulpicius, Severus, went to see them, undergoing on the way the severest toils and dangers, and
brought back reports of mingled truth and falsehood.
Travelling in those days was a labour, if not of necessity,
then surely of love.   Palladius, for instance, found it
impossible to visit the Upper Thebaid, and Syene, and
that 'infinite multitude of monks, whose fashions of life
no one would believe, for they surpass human life ; who
to this day raise the dead, and walk upon the waters like
Peter ; and whatsoever the Saviour did by the holy
apostles, he does now by them.   But because it would be
very dangerous if we went beyond Lyco (Lycopolis),' on
account of the inroad of robbers, he 'could not see those
saints.' "

The holy men and women of whom he wrote, Palladius tells us, he could not see without undergoing infinite
hardships ; seven times he and his companions were
nearly lost.   Once they walked through the Desert five
days and nights, and were almost exhausted by hunger
and thirst.   Again, they fell on rough marshes, where the
sharp sedge wounded their feet, causing intolerable pain,
while they were almost killed with the cold.   Another
time, they sunk up to their waists in the mud, and cried
with David, " I am come into deep mire, where no ground
is."   Another time, they waded for four days through
the flood of the Nile by paths almost washed away.
Another time, they met robbers on the sea-shore, coming
to Diobros, and were chased by them for ten miles.

Another time, their boat was nearly capsized, and they themselves almost drowned, in crossing the Nile. Another time, in the marshes of Mareotis, "where paper grows," they were cast on a little desert island, and remained three days and nights in the open air, amid great cold and showers, for it was the season of Epiphany. The eighth peril, says Palladius, is hardly worth mentioning; but once, when they went to Nitria, they came on a great hollow, in which many crocodiles had remained when the waters retired from the fields. Three of them lay along the banks; and the monks went up to them, thinking them dead, whereon the crocodiles rushed at them. But when they called aloud on the Lord God, "the monsters, as if turned away by an angel," dashed headlong into the water; while they pursued their way to Nitria, meditating on the words of Job: "Seven times shall he deliver thee from trouble; and in the eighth there shall no evil touch thee."

Through such perils and tribulation did Christian men and women persevere until they reached the rocky wilderness of the Thebaid, where they found asylums in the caves and hollows of the mountains, and by their example helped to found those monastic communities which afterwards extended into Europe, and influenced so largely the course of European history during the Middle Ages.

Most of the grottoes of the Thebaid, however, would seem to have been excavated entirely by human handiwork; they are found in the face of a mountain which looks out upon the Nile, and spread along a range of fifteen to twenty leagues.

At the first glance it is not difficult to perceive that
these grottoes were originally excavated for materials to
be employed in the construction of the neighbouring
towns; or rather, perhaps, in that of the Pyramids. In
truth, the blocks removed from these vast quarries have
left huge, dim, low cavities, forming a kind of enfilade
without symmetry and without order. The roofs of these
cavities, low and unequal, are supported at intervals
by pillars which have evidently been left intact for this
special purpose by the workmen.

What, then, are called the grottoes and caverns of the
Lower Thebaid seem to have been neither more nor less
than *quarries;* and history comes forward to prove that
such was really their origin. You may read in the lively
and picturesque pages of Herodotus, that King Cléopas
employed a hundred thousand men for ten years in opening up quarries in the mountains westward of the Nile;
and that for another decade the same or another hundred
thousand unfortunate labourers were occupied in raising
a pyramid of the stone thus obtained, which was white
and soft while fresh from the quarry, but gradually hard-
ened and acquired a brownish colour on exposure to the
air. At a later period, the Ptolemean successors of Alexander on the throne of Egypt, and, after them, the
Romans, drew from these same quarries an immense
amount of stone for the erection of their various edifices.

We find in the rock-caves of the Thebaid regular holes
dug out of the solid rock. They measure about six feet
in length, by ten feet in width, and it is supposed were
used as tombs.

We remark, too, in the roofs of each gloomy grotto,
numerous very small cells, with doors and windows not

above a foot square. Some writers have concluded that these were the places of retreat or asylum of the devout solitaries.

If Herodotus may be credited, the grottoes of the Thebaid date back to a very distant antiquity.

THE CATACOMBS OF ALEXANDRIA.

It is a common belief—perhaps we should rather say, a vulgar error—that no catacombs exist beyond the limits of Christianity and Rome. But, from a very early period, the Egyptians, as well as many other nations, were in the habit of entrusting their dead to the care of Mother Earth; and, moreover, of collecting them in a common place of sepulture. It is true that we must be careful here to distinguish the hypogeum from the catacomb. The hypogea were private places of interment, which admitted only the members of a limited number of families. The catacombs were more modern in origin, and were common burial-places or cemeteries, open to all who had lived in the same religious faith.

But even among the catacombs, some are heathen and others Christian. Thus, the city of Alexandria possesses both heathen and Christian catacombs.

The heathen catacombs of Alexandria, mentioned by Strabo under the name of *Necropolis*,* are situated beyond the western gate of the old city. As Strabo and Athenaeus inform us, the approach to them was formerly very bright and pleasant, lying through a maze of gardens and vineyards. They are of great extent, and cut partly in a ridge of sandy calcareous stone, and partly

* Strabo, "Geography," book xvii., c. 1.

in the calcareous rock opposite the sea, with which they communicate by narrow vaults. The largest of them lies about 3830 yards to the west of the so-called Pompey's Pillar. Their style of decoration is Greek; and a Doric entablature and mouldings in one of the chambers are executed with the most artistic purity.

THE SERAPEION, OR TEMPLE OF SERAPIS.

We must not quit the interesting subject of Egyptian antiquities without a reference to the *Serapeion,* whose remains have been discovered only within the last few years.

The Serapeion, situated in the vast Necropolis of Memphis, is a long subterranean gallery, consecrated as a temple or sepulchre to the god Apis or Serapis, the supreme divinity, whose visible representation was the sacred ox, or the bull Apis. In this gallery, after its death, the honoured animal was pompously interred. The word *Serapeion,* in fact, explains itself; *Serapis* meaning " the dead Apis."

The Egyptian Apis, or the divine bull, was worshipped as a symbol of Osiris. He was attended by a retinue of priests, and sacrifices of red oxen were offered to him. All his changes of appetite, all his movements, and his choice of places, were carefully watched as oracular. He was not allowed to live longer than five-and-twenty years. If he died of natural causes before that age, his body was embalmed as a mummy, and interred in the subterranean tombs. Otherwise, he was secretly put to death, and buried by the priests in a sacred well. A new type of divinity was then sought for. It was necessary that the animal selected should be marked with a white square

on his forehead, an eagle on his back, and a knob like a
cantharus under his tongue. When discovered, he was
conveyed with great pomp to Nilopolis; where he remained for forty days, attended by naked women, prior
to his removal to Memphis.

BRONZES OF THE EGYPTIAN GOD APIS.

Herodotus tells us that, after the defeat of the Persian
army in the Libyan desert, Cambyses returned to this
city (524 B.C.), to find its inhabitants rejoicing at the discovery of a calf marked with the mystic characters, which
showed its supernatural origin. Supposing the public joy
to have arisen from his own defeat, Cambyses summoned
the magistrates of Memphis before him. They endeavoured to pacify the tyrant by relating the discovery of
Apis; but he immediately condemned them to death as
liars. He then ordered Apis and his priests to be brought

into his presence : he would soon know, he exclaimed, whether a tame god had really come to dwell in Egypt. Drawing his dagger, he stabbed the calf in the thigh, and sentenced the priests to be scourged. His subsequent disasters and lunatic excesses were supposed by the Egyptians to be the penalty inflicted by the gods for this sacrilegious act.

In the Serapeion were preserved the mummies of all the sacred bulls from the reign of Amenophis III. (about 1400 B.C.). The year of the king's reign in which each Apis was born, the year when he was received as the representative of the god, the year when he was solemnly interred among his predecessors, were all set forth on a monumental tablet over his remains ; and as these tablets range from the nineteenth dynasty to the epoch of Ptolemaeus II. (177 B.C.), their chronological value is considerable. The most important of these tablets, which number about twelve hundred, have been removed to the Louvre at Paris.

The mummies are arranged in two principal corridors, of which the smaller is the more ancient. The second and larger appears to have been begun in the reign of Psammetichus I., and his fifty-third year ; and contains some magnificent sarcophagi of granite, most of which, unfortunately, have been violated, and are now empty. The paintings with which they were embellished have so faded in a majority of instances as to be unintelligible.*

* M. Mariette, " Serapeum de Memphis " (4to. Paris, 1856). It is necessary to caution the young reader that though M. Mariette may, perhaps, be trusted for his *facts*, no credence must be given to his *deductions*, which are mostly extravagant and unfounded.

II

Ancient Hindustan.

INTRODUCTION.

SUBTERRANEAN temples are not confined to Egypt; magnificent remains exist in Hindustan, where, as in Egypt, religion was the fundamental principle of social organization.

It was to be expected, moreover, that in Hindustan, as in every other land where prevailed the *cultus* of Nature—that gloomy religion, the declared enemy of Light, which was based upon human sacrifices—the temples in which these awful rites were celebrated should be sunken deep in the earth,—deep in obscurity and darkness.

Now, the subterranean temples we meet with in Hindustan differ essentially, and in many points of view, from the Egyptian speos. Their places and elevation are alike. The Egyptian division of a pronaos, naos, and sekos are nowhere found in India. Moreover, the roof of the Indian *speos* is nearly always shaped like an ogival vault, a form unknown in Egypt. Then, again, the Indian columns are always planted on pedestals of the same dimensions as their shafts, and every figure is of fantastic, almost Satanic character. The Egyptian

(709)   4

columns, on the contrary, have *no* pedestals; and the statues accompanying them are always distinguished by their calm and monumental air, their noble and serene physiognomy. Finally, the Egyptian excavations are much deeper and more richly decorated; they belong also to a remoter antiquity; for, as we have seen, the majority of them date as far back as the fourteenth or fifteenth century before Christ, while the most ancient in Hindustan are not older than five or six hundred years before the Christian era.

To the worship of Brahma, and in part to that of Buddha, are consecrated the subterranean temples of Hindustan; the sculptures adorning them all represent subjects borrowed from the same mythology.

These temples were unknown to Europeans down to a comparatively recent period.

Prior to the eighteenth century, says Schlegel,* our European travellers had visited but a small number of the temples and edifices of ancient Hindustan: those, namely, situated on the islands, as at Elephanta and Salsette; or on the coast, as at Mahavalipuram. The majority of the Indian monuments, adds the same writer, have been known to us only in the last half-century.

Since that epoch a great change has taken place. The British Government has facilitated scientific inquiry, and its officials have laboured to become acquainted with the monuments and memorials of the great empire entrusted to their charge: and, therefore, if we do not know *all* the temples of Hindustan, assuredly we know the most remarkable and important; and we may now assert, that

* Schlegel, "On the Growth and Actual Condition of our Knowledge of India" (*Almanach de Berlin*, 1831).

' all the gigantic and remarkable monuments bequeathed
 us by the ancient world, it is India which offers us the
ost extraordinary and the most astounding.   Veltheim,
hose explorations were conducted under official sanction,
 even of opinion that they greatly surpass the works of
gyptian architecture in the artistic skill with which
ey are executed, as in the grandeur and boldness with
hich they were designed.

The Brahmins ascribe to these temples an antiquity
hich it is difficult, nay, impossible to admit.   One thing
 certain, however,—that they belong to the primitive
ges of Indian history, when the people were unfettered
 an alien despotism, and that the period of their con-
ruction must have been preceded by centuries of a very
lvanced civilization.   In any case, their grand, and mar-
ellous, and colossal conception, as well as the delicacy
id richness of their details, prove them to have been the
ork of a great number of successive generations, impelled
 a feeling of intense devotion.

The subterranean temples of Hindustan are all com-
·ised within a region of about eight hundred French
agues in extent—a region stretching to the northern
onfines of Hindustan, and even from beyond the Indus,
 Bamian, and the southernmost islands.

The most ancient, by the consent of the best authorities,
that of the island of Elephanta, or Elephant Island.

———

TEMPLE OF ELEPHANTA.

The island of Elephanta, the *Gharipoor* of the natives,
es off the western coast of the Deccan, in the Gulf of
ombay or Sea of Oman, at a distance of seven miles

east of the city of Bombay.   Its name is derived, we are told, from a huge stone elephant which formerly stood on the shore.

Its subterranean temple is formed in the interior of a

ENTRANCE TO THE TEMPLE OF ELEPHANTA

grotto excavated high up in a double-peaked mountain, which rises rapidly from the coast.

To reach the temple, we climb a flight of three or four hundred steps, cut out, almost precipitously, in the mountain-side ; this flight conducts to a narrow terrace, whence we obtain one of the most glorious sea-prospects imaginable.   Here opens the main entrance of the grotto ; two massive pillars support it, and divide it into three principal gates, through which we penetrate into a vast and mysterious enclosure, measuring 130 feet in length, 123 feet in breadth, and 18 feet in height.

As the temple is lighted only from the side, by the courts which flank it on the east and west, it takes some time for our eyes to grow accustomed to its semi-obscurity.

hen the shadow is somewhat dissipated, we are struck,
the first place, by the regular and symmetrical aspect
the sixteen grooved columns which support the level
of of this vast hall, and divide it into three naves.
ese columns—originally twenty-six in number, but the
nainder were destroyed by the Portuguese—are about
hteen feet in height:
ey are surmounted by
mispherical capitals.
The general effect of
is sombre enclosure,
th its singular archi-
:ture and its long
w of pillars, is very
e and very impres-
'e, despite some ir-
gularities of detail.
The walls, as well as

GREAT HALL—TEMPLE OF ELEPHANTA.

e pillars, are completely covered with sculptures illus-
tive of the life of Siva, the god to whom the temple is
nsecrated. By the side of Siva you may see Parvati,
s wife; Ganessa and Cartik, his two sons; next Kailasa,
the council of the gods, the Dhagob, and the ornament
the lotus. The figures stand out boldly from the rock,
d astonish the spectator by their gigantic dimensions
d the variety of their attitudes.

In the centre stands a gigantic representation of the
indu Trinity (Brahma, Siva, and Vishnu), cut out of
e solid rock, and surrounded by colossal guardians under
e most varied forms. Two lions originally were planted
· it; but these have been removed to the entrance of
e of the numerous corridors which communicate with

the principal hall, and which is thenceforth designated the
" Court of Lions."

Much that is interesting may be seen in these various
corridors, the walls of which are decorated with remarkable sculptures.

After having indulged to the full his surprise and
admiration, the visitor will be unable to repress a feeling
of indignation at the injuries almost daily inflicted on

INTERIOR OF THE TEMPLE OF ELEPHANTA.

this celebrated monument of Indian antiquity.   A corre-
spondent of *The Times*, who visited the rock-temple of
Elephanta in 1864, complains in strong language of the
irreverent and destructive curiosity of tourists, and especially, we regret to say, of English tourists.   The most
delicate sculptures have undoubtedly suffered for many
years from the violence of the Portuguese ; just as in

England itself some of the most admirable monuments of Gothic architecture have been despoiled by the sincere but mistaken zeal of iconoclastic Puritans. Unfortunately, what Portuguese fanaticism commenced has been rapidly completed by plundering collectors and ignorant amateurs.

THE COURT OF LIONS—ELEPHANTA.

The façade of the gigantic group of the Hindu Trinity is covered with the names of visitors scrawled in pencil, written in ink, or rudely engraved, either by the sailor's knife or the soldier's sword. To break off a nose, provided it is not done for the mere pleasure of destruction but to indulge a collector's mania, is regarded as an act almost honourable, and dictated by national sentiment.   To eat and drink upon rude tables in this desolate sanctuary of the gods of the old time does not satisfy the thirst for novelty recently developed in " young England," whose half-Americanized representatives would take no pleasure in their lively picnics if they did not whet their appetites with the atmosphere of marvellous monuments.   But this is not all.   There was at work on the island, some few years since,—and its operations may still be continued,— a company employing several thousands of coolies, under the auspices of the firm of Messrs. Nicholas.   Another designs to connect the islands of Elephanta and Bombay by a railway and bridges.   Perhaps, before this is carried out, a proposal will be brought forward to transport the sculptures of the temple to South Kensington, or to the Victoria Museum, Bombay.   But the true, the fitting, the only place for these precious objects, for these memorials of ancient art, is the place where the ancient science and ancient devotion called them into existence,—where they are mirrored in the blue waves or caressed by the shadow of the palm-trees.   There they become for the reflecting mind the tangible images of the antique and solemn reveries of the sages of the mysterious Eastern World, that world of which, notwithstanding all our efforts, we as yet know so very little ; they become both an enigma and a lesson, though abandoned now as the temple of a decaying creed, and deserted as its altars.

We may hope, however, that these monuments will be more reverently treated, since the Indian Government appointed a commission to provide for the due custody and preservation of Indian antiquities.

THE TEMPLES OF ELLORA.

The temple of Elephanta, as we have said, we take to be the most ancient rock-temple in the Indian peninsula; but the most remarkable in all other respects, and espeially in the magnitude of their proportions, are the celerated subterranean temples of Ellora, near the city of that name, or about twenty miles north west of Douletabad, apital of the province of Aurungabad, and nearly in the entre of Hindustan.

These monuments have been excavated by the hand of nan in a belt of sandstone mountains, which extends in horse-shoe shape over an area of upwards of five miles, with its concave face towards the village of Rosah. They orm subterranean galleries not less than two leagues in xtent, which, in certain places, are built in stories communicating with one another. The imagination recoils ghast at the immense patience and labour which have een expended on these colossal excavations, and the culptures of every kind so profusely decorating them. The rare perfection of certain portions, and the ruder work of others, clearly demonstrate that they have been xcuted by thousands of artists labouring successively in he descending course of centuries.

As for the origin of the temples of Ellora, it is almost nknown. Sir Charles Malet relates several traditions, each f which differs as to the king who founded them. The Moslems attribute them to the Râdjâ El, who flourished bout nine hundred years ago; the Hindus date them as ar back as Êlora, who reigned in the Dwaparâ-Youga, or nore than seven thousand nine hundred years, according o Hindu chronology; finally, the Purânas speak of a

King Ela, otherwise called Pourouravas, who dates from
the commencement of the Indian monarchy.   Nothing is
less certain than all these traditions ; but we may venture
to affirm that the sculptures engraved upon these monuments assign to them a much more recent date.   According to Gailhabaud, we must not accord to them a greater
antiquity than two thousand years ; and Mr. Fergusson is
of opinion that the last of the series at Ellora was completed by Indradyumna.

Among the monuments of Ellora, the most beautiful
and the most finished is the *Kailasa,* or *Kelaça,* so called
to the present day by the Hindus themselves.

This exceedingly complex structure covers an area of
about 400 feet in length by 190 feet in breadth.   It has
not been constructed like those around it—that is to say,
excavated subterraneously ; it is carved out of the live
rock, and completely detached from the mountain ; and
though all its parts form but one and the same block,
though it is composed entirely of the single rock in which
it has been sculptured, it has, nevertheless, all the appearance of an edifice built stone upon stone.

The Kailasa, therefore, not being included in the cate-
gory of rock-temples, properly so called, we should have
passed it by unnoticed, if it were possible to speak of the
temples of Ellora without mentioning the most remarkable and celebrated.   Our account of it must, however,
be brief.

We enter the Kailasa by a gateway of granite, and
having crossed its threshold, pass through a magnificent
portico into a kind of court, about 230 feet by 100 feet

wide, with walls 140 feet high. This court, says Ramée, being wholly carved out of the rock, may be compared to a magic quarry of stones surrounded and crowned on all sides by mountain-summits, rather than to a work produced by the hand and skill of man.

On issuing from the portico, we first cross a small bridge to a square pavilion, which contains the chapel or sanctuary of Nandi, the companion of Siva. Next we traverse a second bridge, and finally arrive at the principal temple. This, the greatest monolithic temple known, is supported by enormous square pilasters, disposed in four rows; those at the angles, and at the circumference, twenty in number, are themselves supported by elephants, which seem to raise on their backs the enormous mass, and communicate to it motion and life.

The great temple, 500 feet in circumference, is flanked by porches, terraces, basins, and chapels; and the court which surrounds it on every side is decorated with obelisks and gigantic elephants. The walls are enriched with thousands of statues and bas-reliefs.

The mind is struck with amazement when it reflects on the immense and protracted labour which these interminable constructions must necessarily have entailed.

To raise the Pantheon, says Captain Seely,* the Parthenon of Athens, St. Peter's at Rome, or St. Paul's at London, must have cost both science and toil; we know, however, in what way each great edifice was begun, carried on, and completed. But what we cannot imagine is, that any body of men, let them be as numerous and as well provided as you choose with the means necessary for the realization of their conception, should attack a natural

* Captain Seely, "Travels to Ellora," &c.

rock, in some places 800 feet high, excavate it, carve it out with hammer and chisel, and rear such a temple as this, a veritable Pantheon! with long dim galleries, a vast court, and an infinite number of sculptures and ornaments. No; this work soars beyond the range of imagination, and the mind loses itself in surprise and admiration.

Let us now pass on to the completely subterranean temples excavated in the mountain which serves as an enclosure for the Kailasa; these are "more germane" to the subject of the present volume.

One of the most interesting, not so much in its dimensions as in the elegance and originality of its execution, is the temple or house of Bisma Kurm.*

This temple is excavated in the rock at a depth of about one hundred and sixty-six feet. It consists of a long gallery, with a circular ceiling, separated longitudinally into three aisles by two rows of twenty-eight octagonal pillars, which are about three feet in circumference.

The statue of the god, represented as the primitive architect, is enthroned in a niche; at his feet are two lions, images of power and force; by his side are two of his servants, one of whom holds a lotus-flower, the symbol of creation and production, as well as a small staff representing the might of sovereignty; the other is hanging a triangular "level" on a species of column. Above Bisma Kurm glows an eye, emblematical of penetration and ordaining wisdom; and above this eye is placed a workman's plummet, which, descending upon a horizontal line,

* Bisma Kurm, or Vishwa Karma, is the personification of Buddh considered as the primitive architect.

forms two right angles, the absolute principles of all kinds of creation, formation, and regular construction.

It is probable that this remarkable temple was reared in the centuries immediately preceding the Christian era.

INTERIOR OF TEMPLE—ELLORA.

Another interesting excavation is that of Para-Lanka, the entrance of which is placed on the upper stage of a two-tier gallery. Access to it is obtained by a flight of seven-and-twenty steps.

The perfectly dry nature of the rock, which allows no infiltration to pass through, and does not retain a trace of humidity, has preserved the beautiful designs painted on the stucco of the ceiling of the cavern, and representing subjects borrowed from the Hindu mythology. Enor-

mous pillars, covered with carved work from top to
bottom, support this platform, which would still shine
out in the original splendour of its costly decorations, had
not the barbarian's hand interfered to deface them.   The
Moslem soldiers of the Mongolian emperor, Aurungzebe,
intended, in the name of Mohammed, to annihilate the
superstitious labours of the ancient Brahmins.   Happily
the work of destruction demanded so much time and so
much work that they abandoned it.   Hence the Hindus
have not failed to concoct a miracle, and they pretend
that Siva deigned to interfere on behalf of his temple.
The intervention of Siva, however, was not carried so far
as to neutralize the ill effects of smoke.   The soldiers of
Aurungzebe would seem to have performed their cooking
operations under the very nose of god and goddess, and
the smoke has blackened the ceiling, and injured nearly
every painting ; enough remains to make us regret what
has perished.

On issuing from the grotto of Para-Lanka, we find ourselves under a peristyle, whence the gaze embraces the
whole external portion of the monuments of Ellora.

TEMPLES OF SALSETTE.

The island of Salsette, or Salcette,—in Hindu, *Djhalta,*
—lies to the north of the island of Bombay, with which
it is connected by a causeway.

It contains a considerable number of subterranean
temples.   The most remarkable and the most celebrated
are those of Kennery, situated on the north-eastern shore
of the island, near the fortress of Tanna.

The temples of Kennery are supported against the

ro slopes of a mountain-chain, which extends in the
ape of a horse-shoe, and are so considerable in number
at they form a complete troglodyte town. They com-
unicate with one another by flights of steps, which lead
the summit of the mountain. They are not all of the
me dimensions.

The largest is especially interesting and curious, from
s connection with the history of Buddhism, and with
e power of the Brahmins in the Deccan. It measures
5 feet in length, by 36 feet in breadth. Two rows of
lumns separate it into three aisles, of which the prin-
pal terminates in a hemicycle; thus exhibiting the exact
ound-plan of the old Roman basilica, afterwards adapted
the early Christian Church. In the hemicycle is placed
e Dhagob, or Dagoba, that mysterious pillar of Buddh-
m which Bishop Heber, in 1825, supposed to be the
mbol of the Lingam, and whose true signification has
nce been explained by Wilhelm von Humboldt in his
ork on the Karvi language as used in the island of
va. The square pillars of the raised portico, through
hich we enter this subterranean temple, are covered
ith long inscriptions.

The inscriptions extant in this temple, and in the other
xcavations of the island of Salsette, range from 150 B.C.
wn to 1400 A.D. The later are written in Arabic and
ersian, and relate to the Moslem worship. When they
all all have been read and interpreted, a new light
ill be thrown upon the history of Hindustan.

The temples of Kennery, as we have said, are not the
ly temples to be found in the island of Salsette. There
e others not wanting in interest, though our space pre-
ents us from describing them. One is a hundred paces

in length, by forty in width ; and consists of a considerable number of galleries, flights of stairs, halls, and artificial basins for the reception of rain-water, to be used in the numerous lavatory processes of the Hindu *cultus*.

GROTTOES OF KARLI.

The famous grottoes of Karli are situated in the chain of the Western Ghauts, between Bombay and Poona, opposite the fort of Lohaghow, and not far from Khandalla.

From Dr. Norman Macleod* we borrow the following graphic description of their position and character :—

"In about an hour from the time of starting," he says, "we reached the platform leading to the famous caves. 'But what caves?' my reader very naturally asks. In reply, I beg to inform him that long ago, before the beginning of the Christian era, that form of religion called Buddhism was supreme in India. It is now extinct in Hindustan ; but in Ceylon, Burmah, China, and Tibet, it has even yet a greater number of followers than any other system of religious belief can claim in the world. Some centuries before Christ, the Buddhists waged great ecclesiastical wars with the Brahmins and their caste system. They had then in India, as they have now wherever they exist, their churches, with internal arrangements not unlike our own, and their monasteries, with hordes of monks, who practised celibacy, shaved their crowns, and lived by alms. The caves of Karli are the finest of several fine specimens which survive of Buddhist early architecture, dating back as far perhaps

* "Peeps at the Far East," in *Good Words* for 1809, pp. 258, 259.

as the first century. They tell their own story regarding this strange and venerable body. To come suddenly on such massive and imposing architecture in a wild recess of rocks and brushwood, is in itself impressive, and more especially so when associated with thoughts of the vast antiquity of the system of belief which they represent, and of its still powerful influence on so large a portion of the human race. The details of this caverned hill are also most striking. In a recess on each side of the doorway there is a most original, and to me most appropriate, architectural ornament,—elephants in bold relief, fronting the spectator with their heads and trunks, as if bearing up on their huge and powerful backs the mass of sculptured rock above. The interior of the 'church,' too, is very impressive. The centre aisle has fifteen pillars, twenty-five feet high on each side, separating it from the two side aisles. At the end there is a dome-shaped building, called a Dagoba,* like a high altar, within an apse surrounded by seven pillars. The roof is arched with ribs of timber, probably as old as the excavation. There is no light except from the great open window above, through which it falls directly upon the 'altar,' leaving the rest of the cathedral in shadow. The length is 186 feet, the breadth 45 feet, and the height 45 feet.

"Around the church are the various halls and cells of a monastery, which are also cut out of the living rock. There are three stories; and the ascent from the lower to some of the higher being interrupted, the strong arms of guides are required to push one up, as through a wide chimney, and across rather awkward gaps. The upper

* From *dhatu*, relic; and *gabba* or *garba*, a shrine or womb.

story is a noble *vihara* or hall, with an open balcony or verandah supported by stone pillars. From this there is a commanding view. There is a raised *dais* at the end of the hall, as if meant to be occupied by the superior of the monastery. Around it are the small cells of the monks,—each having had a door, probably of stone. Within is the narrow stone bed on which the ascetics lay. On the walls are sculptures,—figures of saints, with the halo round their heads. I was very thankful," says our authority, in conclusion, " to see this dead monument which so vividly recalled a living past."

The resemblance of the cave at Karli to a Christian church is very great. It has its nave, and its side aisles, terminating in an apse or semi-dome, round which the aisle is carried. The general dimensions of the interior are 126 feet from the entrance to the back wall, by 45 feet 7 inches in width from wall to wall. The side aisles, however, are very much narrower than in Christian churches, the central one being 25 feet 7 inches, so that the others are only 10 feet wide, including the thickness of the pillars. The height, from the floor to the apex, is 42 to 45 feet.

An elaborate architectural description of this singular Buddhist sanctuary has been drawn up by Mr. Fergusson.* The interior, he says, is as solemn and grand as any interior can be, and the mode of lighting the most perfect; one individual volume of light coming through a single opening overhead at a very favourable angle, and falling directly on the altar or principal object in the building, leaving the rest in comparative obscurity. The effect is considerably heightened by the thick and closely-

* Fergusson, " Illustrated Handbook of Architecture," vol. l., pp. 26, 27.

set columns that divide the three aisles from one another, as they suffice to prevent the boundary walls from ever being seen ; and, as there are no openings in the walls, the view between the pillars is practically unlimited.

Of these pillars there are two rows, and fifteen in each row ; each has a tall base, an octagonal shaft, and a richly ornamented capital, on which kneel two elephants, each bearing two figures—generally a man and a woman, but sometimes two females, all very much better executed than such ornaments usually are. The seven pillars behind the altar are plain octagonal piers, without either base or capital ; and the four under the entrance gallery differ considerably from those at the sides. These sculptures on the capitals, remarks Mr. Fergusson, supply the place usually occupied by frieze and cornice in Grecian architecture ; and in other examples, plain painted surfaces occupy the same space. Above this springs the roof, semicircular in general section, but somewhat stilted at the sides, so as to make its height greater than the semi-diameter. It is ornamented even at this day by a series of wooden ribs, probably coeval with the excavation, which prove beyond the shadow of a doubt that the roof is not a copy of a masonry arch, but of some sort of timber construction, which we cannot now very well understand.

Immediately beneath the apsidal semi-dome, and nearly at the exact spot which the altar would occupy in Christian churches, stands the shrine,—in this instance, " a plain dome slightly stilted on a circular drum." As it is now without ornament, and has no mortices for wood-work, it probably was originally plastered and painted ; or it may have been adorned with tapestry.

which some of the sculptured representations would lead us to suppose was the usual mode of ornamenting these altars.

Opposite this is the entrance, under a gallery exactly resembling our "rood-loft," and consisting of three doorways, one leading to the centre, and one to each of the side aisles; and over the gallery the whole end of the hall is open, forming one great window, through which all the light is admitted. This great window is arched in the shape of a horse-shoe, and simply ornamented. The outer porch is considerably wider than the body of the building, being fifty-two feet in width, and is closed in front by a screen composed of two stout octagonal pillars, without either base or capital, supporting what is now a plain mass of rock, though it was once ornamented by a wooden gallery, which formed the principal ornament of the façade. Above this a dwarf colonnade or attic of four columns between pilasters admitted light to the great window; and this again was surmounted by a wooden cornice or ornament of some sort, though we cannot now restore it, as only the mortices remain that attached it to the rock.

Still further in advance of this stands the "Lion-Pillar," a plain shaft with thirty-two flutes, or rather "faces," surmounted by a kind of Ionic capital, supporting four lions. A similar pillar probably stood on the opposite side, but it has either fallen, or been removed to make way for the little temple that now occupies its place.

We subjoin a comparative table of some of the principal rock-temples in the Western Ghauts, with their supposed dates :—

	Length.	Width.	Probable Age.
	Ft. In.	Ft. In.	
Karli	126 0	45 7	1st century after Christ.
Ajunta (No. 10)	94 6	41 3	1st century after Christ.
Ajunta (No. 9)	45 0	23 0	2nd or 3rd century.
Ajunta (No. 19)	46 4	23 7	5th century.
Ajunta (No. 26)	66 1	36 3	9th or 10th century
Bisma Kurm, at Ellora...	85 1	43 0	7th or 8th century.
Kannori	88 6	39 10	9th or 10th century.

TEMPLES OF AJAYANTI, OR AJUNTA.

As is shown in the preceding table, the tenth cave

EXTERIOR OF THE CHAITYA CAVE—AJUNTA.

mple at Ajunta (a Sanskrit word, signifying the " im-
regnable defile "), is next in size to that of Karli. There

are a considerable number of those sanctuaries, but as they closely resemble each other, and the temple of Karli, in architectural character, it is needless to describe them. The principal difference is, that in some of the caves the pillars are octagonal. They are not all, however, equally perfect in execution; and of the latest (No. 26), Mr. Fergusson remarks, that its sculptural arrangements show such a degenerate tendency towards modern Hinduism, as to denote that the style was at its last gasp when the cave was commenced.

TEMPLES OF PANDOU-LENA.

In the same province as those of Karli and Ajunta— that is, Aurungabad, in the Deccan—and at about two hours' journey south-west of the fort of Nassouk, are situated the rock-temples of Pandou-Lena.

TEMPLE OF MHAR.

The province of Aurungabad is very rich in Buddhist memorials; and the temple of Mhar, near the fortress of the same name, is not one of the least interesting. It lies at no great distance from Poona and Sattara, on the western slope of the North Ghauts, in the upper valley of the river Bancut or Sawuty.

This temple, in its general features, resembles that of Salsette. The principal hall, the walls of which are smooth and unadorned, measures about 60 feet in length, 30 feet in width, and $10\frac{1}{2}$ feet in height. At its eastern extremity is an enthroned idol, cut out of the rock; and on each side of this idol are two much smaller statues, and the fragments of two figures of animals. The light is admitted into this grotto through a colonnade.

GROTTOES OF PANCH-PANDOU.

The grottoes of Panch-Pandou (the five Pandous) are situated near the small town of Bang, in the province of Malva; they are four in number, but the northern is the only one in a state of tolerable preservation.

THE GROTTOES OF DHOUMNAR.

Colonel Todd has explored at Dhoumnar, in the north of the province of Malva, as many as one hundred and seventy subterranean passages leading to a number of temples and monasteries, the whole forming a great subterranean city. Though these temples are less majestic than those of Ellora, Salsette, and Karli, Colonel Todd is, nevertheless, of opinion that they belong to a very remote antiquity. In truth, they are rough, rugged, but bold in conception and execution. The inscriptions have been almost wholly defaced; only a few remains of the characters being extant, and these are undecipherable.

GROTTOES OF BAMIAN.

Bamian is situated in the wildest region of the Hindu-Koosh, not far from the source of the Surkhab, one of the affluents on the left or southern bank of the Djihoun (the ancient *Oxus*), about 52 miles from Cabool.

The innumerable grottoes which occur here are, for the most part, mere quarried excavations, without architecture and without ornaments. In some the roof forms a kind of dome, and at the place from which it springs is set a small decorated frieze.

These caves were described as early as the latter part of the sixth century by Abul-Fazel :—

"In the heart of the mountain of Bamian," he says, "are twelve thousand cavities or grottoes cut in the rock, with ornaments and mouldings in stucco. They were used by the natives of the country for an asylum in winter, and are called *Summij* (caves): enormous figures are found in them, as of a man eighty ells in height, a woman fifty, and a child fifteen. In one of these grottoes you may see an embalmed corpse (or mummy), whose origin is unknown to the natives, and they hold it in high honour."

Ritter is of opinion that these monuments date from the epoch of the introduction of Buddhism into Hindustan ; that is, from five to six centuries before our era. The native tradition affirms that they are the work of a king named Joulal, and the locality is known as Ghoul-goula or Ghalgala.

Some very extraordinary myths are connected with these grottoes. In one of them, it is said, the famous Vyasa composed the Vedas,—those mystic expositions of the early religion of India, in which religion, morality, truth, and fable are so curiously blended. In another, so runs the story, a mother lost her child, and did not recover him until ten years had elapsed. Some historians point out one of the caverns as for a long period the residence of the famous Mani, the Hindu heresiarch, who flourished towards the close of the third century. And to conclude : Ritter believes that at Bamian must be placed the cave rendered eternally celebrated by the fable of Prometheus. In support of his opinion he brings forward a statement in Quintus Curtius, book vii. c. 24. In the legend of Vishnu, we also read of a Pramat'hesa ("lord of the five senses"), who, having audaciously defied the gods, was devoured by an eagle or vulture, named Garuda.

III

Ancient Greece.

INTRODUCTION.

N the religious history of ancient Greece an important part was played by its caverns and natural grottoes.

Thus Porphyry says, in his treatise "De Antro Nympharum" (c. xx.), that before the older races had built up temples to their divinities, the earliest inhabitants of Hellas had consecrated to purposes of religious worship the "caves and antres vast" (σπήλαια καὶ ἄντρα); as, in the island of Crete to Zeus, in Arcadia to Artemis and Pan, in Naxos to Dionysos; and wherever adoration was paid to Mithra, the sun-god, he was also honoured with sacrifices in subterranean sanctuaries.

These were the mysteries, still celebrated, during the first two or three centuries of Christianity, in the shadow and darkness of gloomy caverns, which the Christian Fathers so vehemently and so justly condemned.

THE CRETAN LABYRINTH.

Both in the history and mythology of Greece we meet

with the traces of a great number of vast halls or galleries,—galleries with innumerable ramifications, and all underground,—to which the name of "labyrinth" was given, and on whose model, at a later date, certain edifices were constructed.

The most famous of these labyrinths is that of Crete, which the fable of the Minotaur has rendered familiar to every classical student.

It was an ancient quarry, situated near Knôssos, and, according to tradition, was designed and excavated by Daedalus.* It was intended, like the rock-tombs of Egypt, for the place of sepulture of the royal family.

We take it for granted that our readers know the fable of the Minotaur; that Cretan monster, half man, half bull, sprung from the supposed connection of Pasiphae, the wife of Minos and daughter of Apollo, with a bull— or, as some say, a certain Cretan warrior, named Taurus. The fable asserts that the monster was immured in the Daedalian labyrinth, and that, every seventh year, the Athenians were compelled to send seven youths and maidens to be devoured by it. Theseus, the great hero of Athens, resolved to release his subjects from this intolerable exaction. Visiting Knôssos, he won the love of Ariadne, daughter of Minos, and was by her provided with a clew of thread, which enabled him to penetrate into the labyrinth and slay the monster.

We know, too, that the hero rewarded the love of Ariadne by carrying her off from Crete, and afterwards abandoning her, while asleep, on the island of Naxos; where Bacchus discovered her, and, out of pity, wedded her.

* See Grote, "History of Greece," L 212–217.

The Minotaur, by our comparative mythologists, is supposed to be the Phoenician symbol of the sun-god, and the labyrinth was probably constructed for purposes connected with his worship. Like the celebrated Egyptian labyrinth, near Lake Moeris, it may, perhaps, have been designed as a symbolical representation of the zodiac and the solar system. Or the tradition may have arisen from the existence of numerous natural caves, which were connected by artificial galleries, and converted into temples. This explanation is the more feasible in that certain ancient writers describe it as "a subterranean cavern," and as "a mountain with a cavern." At all events, no traces of it are now to be detected; nor were any visible in the days of Diodorus and Pliny.

THE CAVE OF TROPHONIUS.

Of the prophetic caverns where the Pythonesses rendered their oracular utterances in the name of some one or other of the deities, no vestiges are extant. But near Livadia, the ancient Lebadeia,—capital of Boeotia,—a great cavern is pointed out as that so celebrated in ancient Greece for its oracles—the cave of Trophonius.

We find in Pausanias* some curious details in reference to this oracle. But, first, we must ask, Who was Trophonius? Little is recorded of his life by ancient writers, but he appears to have been the son, either of Apollo, or of Erginus, King of Orchomenus; and, in conjunction with his brother Agamedes, to have erected many superb palaces and temples, especially the Delphic temple of Apollo, and the treasury of King Hyreius in Boeotia.

* Pausanias, Ἑλλάδος Περιήγησις, ix. 37-39, &c.

Though a skilful architect, he was not an honest man ; and the latter edifice he built in such a manner that, by the removal of a single stone from the outside, he and his brother could enter whenever they chose, and remove whatever they wished.

We may imagine the astonishment of Hyrieus when he discovered that, though his locks and seals remained intact, his treasures diminished daily. To detect the mysterious thief or thieves, he placed some snares about his vessels of silver and gold, and patiently awaited the result. Agamedes entered ; was entrapped ; and Trophonius, to save himself from exposure, and his brother from the tortures he would undergo on being discovered, cut off his head.

This cruel example of promptitude and resolution brought no good fortune to Trophonius. The earth, shortly afterwards, opened beneath his feet and engulfed him at Lebadeia, in the sacred grove which thenceforth bore his name, and at the very spot where was found the fosse called the fosse of Agamedes.

It seems strange that a fratricide should be worshipped as a hero, or that he should be honoured as the inspiration of one of the most celebrated oracles of Greece. But the mythologists aver that the gift of predicting the future in the very excavation where he was swallowed up was bestowed upon him by Apollo, as a reward for the skill with which he had built the temple at Delphos.

According to Pausanias, the oracle was long unknown, and its discovery by the Boeotians took place in the following manner :—

For two years no rain had fallen in Boeotia. In despair, the inhabitants sent deputies from each of their towns to Delphi, to implore Apollo to put an end to the drought. The Pythian ordered them to repair to Trophonius at Lebadeia, assuring them that they would obtain from him a remedy for their ills. Accordingly they went to Lebadeia, but could not find the oracle they sought. During the search, however, Saon, of the town of Acroeplinum, the oldest of all the deputies, caught sight of a swarm of bees, and the thought struck him that he would follow them wherever they flew. Suddenly he saw the bees direct their course towards a mysterious grotto, which he entered with them : the oracle was discovered. It is said that Saon was instructed by Trophonius himself as to the manner in which he should order all things relating to his *cultus*, and to the other ceremonies connected with the oracle.

Whoever desired to consult the oracle was first required to purify himself by spending some days in the sanctuary of the Good Spirit and Good Fortune (ἀγαθοῦ Δαίμονος καὶ ἀγαθῆς Τύχης), to live abstemiously, and to bathe himself in the river Hercyna. He then offered sacrifices to Trophonius and his children, to Apollo, Chronos, King Zeus, Hera Hemiocha, as well as to Demeter Europa, who was said to have nursed Trophonius. During these sacrifices a soothsayer inspected the entrails of the victims, and determined whether Trophonius would receive the supplicant indulgently. In the night preceding his descent into the sacred cave, he had to sacrifice a ram to Agamedes, and then, if the signs were favourable, he was led by two boys of thirteen to the river Hercyna, where he was washed and anointed. The priests next made him drink from the well of Oblivion (Λήθη), that he might forget all his former thoughts; and from the well of

Memory (Μνημοσύνη), that he might recollect the visions about to descend upon him. Then he was permitted to worship a mysterious representation of Trophonius (said to be the work of Daedalus), and being dressed in linen garments with girdles around his body, and wearing a kind of shoes peculiar to the country (κρηπῖδες), he was led into the sanctuary.

Within the sanctuary, which stood on an eminence, above the sacred grove, was a cave, into which the neophyte obtained admittance by means of a ladder. Close to the bottom, in the side of the cave, was a square opening, very skilfully constructed. Here he thrust in his feet, the other parts of his body being drawn into it by some mysterious power, just as a man is carried down by one of those whirlpools which occur in mighty and very rapid rivers. In each hand he held a cake kneaded with honey.

It is unnecessary to point out the impression which such a series of ceremonies must have produced on a credulous imagination, and how prepared it must have been for the reception of any delusion the priests thought proper to practise upon it.

Sometimes, we are told, the future was revealed to the neophyte in visions, sometimes in the prophetic language of a grave and terrible voice. As soon, however, as the deity had made known his fate, or answered his interrogations, he returned through the same opening by which he had entered; whereupon the priests seated him on the throne of Mnemosyne, inquired of him what he had seen and heard, and led him back to the sanctuary of the Good Spirit and Good Fortune.

When he had recovered his reason, and, as Pausanias

drily adds,* his power of laughing, he wrote down his
vision on a little tablet which was dedicated in the
temple.

This experience had formerly so terrible a reputation,
that it became proverbial in Greece to say of any person
who appeared grave and anxious, " He has returned from
the cave of Trophonius."

That it was more frightful than really dangerous, may
be inferred from the statement of Pausanias, that of all
who had descended into the cave, not one had died but
a soldier of the body-guard of Demetrius; and he had
been rash enough to intrude upon the " sacred presence"
without observing any of the ceremonies, and whose real
intention was less to consult the oracle than carry off the
treasures reputed to be stored up in the cave.   It is rea-
sonable to suppose that this impudent plunderer was
slain by the priests.

The oracle of Trophonius was highly esteemed in
Greece; and it is related that, in the wars of Messenia,
the courageous Aristomenes, having lost his buckler while
too ardently pursuing the fugitive Spartans, descended
into the cave of Trophonius, in obedience to the injunctions of the Delphic Pythia, and there recovered the
missing armour, which he afterwards gratefully dedicated
at Lebadeia.   The oracle did not become extinct until a
very late period; and though Sulla and his army plundered the temple, Arigar relates that it was much con-
sulted by the Romans.   In Plutarch's time it was the
only one of the Boeotian oracles which had not become
silent.

---

* Pausanias had descended into the cave, and, consequently, writes with all
the authority of an eye-witness.

Lucian, who lived, it is supposed, in the reigns of Aurelius, Antoninus, and Commodus—that is, from about 120 to 200 A.D.—has gaily jested at the hero and his oracle in one of his celebrated *Dialogues*.*

Trophonius is represented as extolling his oracle to Menippus :—" I am a hero, and I truthfully reveal the events of the future to all who descend into my cave. Thou hast never been at Lebadeia, or thou wouldst not have the least doubt upon the subject."

Menippus replies :—" What sayest thou? To assure myself that thou art dead, as dead as all of us, and to see that thy roguery is the only thing which distinguishes thee, is it necessary to have been at Lebadeia? To have been clothed in a mysterious garment, to have ridiculously carried a cake between my hands, and, thus pleasantly equipped, to have descended to the depths of thy cavern, sliding through a small, dark, and narrow hole? ......But tell me, I pray thee, in the name of thy divine art, what it is to be a hero; for, in truth, I do not at all understand."

Trophonius. A hero is a being who participates in the nature both of gods and men.

Menippus. That is to say, he is neither exactly god nor exactly man, but both at once. In that case, where is now thy divine part?

Trophonius. Uttering oracles in Boeotia.

Menippus. I understand nothing of these oracular distinctions; but at least I am sure of this, that I see you here, Trophonius, one and intact, among the dead.

The good sense of Lucian was in advance of the good

* Lucianus, Νεκρικοὶ Διάλογοι, iii.

sense of the public, which, however, long since did justice
to these absurd superstitions.   And yet dare we affirm,
without the fear of immediate contradiction, that in any
county in England, Wales, or Scotland there are not
hundreds ready to lend a credulous ear to predictions as
absurd as, and less dignified than, the oracles of ancient
Hellas?   A Greek priest was at least a superior impostor
to a gipsy fortune-teller.   He played with the higher
passions and stronger feelings of men, not with their
vulgarest fears and most trivial curiosities.   There was
something romantic and impressive in the apparatus to
which he resorted, and a certain amount of intellectual
force was needed to work it.

The calcareous mountain in which is situated the cave
of Trophonius is tunnelled by a number of other excavations; a circumstance not a little embarrassing to classical tourists in their eager quest after the true sanctuary
of the god.

The majority of travellers, however, seem to agree
with Pouqueville that at the entrance of the genuine and
veritable prophetic grotto is engraved on the rock the
pass-word *Chibolet* (ΧΙΒΟΛΕΤ, or, according to others,
ΖΕΤΣ ΒΟΤΛΑΙΟΣ, Jove the Counsellor),—a fragment of an
inscription of which the remainder is illegible.

A large cross now surmounts the mystical inscription;
and the cave of Trophonius, transformed into a chapel,
continues to be visited by some Christians, who, in their
enthusiasm, are hauled up in a basket attached to the
cord of a pulley.

The grotto is filled with niches for the reception of
offerings; but it is impossible to discover the opening

through which the pilgrims were lowered, nor the secret door through which the priests introduced the secret appliances of their phantasmagoria.

The Sacred Grove, at the foot of the mountain, contained the temple of Trophonius, with a statue of the hero from the wonder-working chisel of Praxiteles; a temple of Demeter Europa; and a statue of Zeus Hyetius (Pluvius) in the open air. Higher up was the oracle; and higher still the hunting-place of Persephone, a large temple of Zeus Basileus (unfinished), a temple of Apollo, and a temple to Chronus, Zeus, and Hera.

The two fountains of Memory and Oblivion were the reputed sources of the Hercyna; but this bright translucent river is simply a continuation of an occasional torrent from Mount Helicon. It is fed, however, by copious streams descending from the castle-hill on the right or eastern bank of the river, and by sources of less importance on the left or west bank, which are named *Krya* (ἡ κρύα, " the cold"), and were probably the fountains made use of by the priests of Trophonius.*

THE GROTTOES OR QUARRIES OF PENTELICUS.

The plain of Athens is bounded on the west by a range of mountains, the northern part of which was anciently called Brilessus, but subsequently Pentelicus, now *Mendeli* or *Penteli*. The marble obtained from this northern part was greatly esteemed by the ancients, and in Athens the principal buildings and statues were sup-

* The actual site of the oracle has not been satisfactorily ascertained. Compare Col. Mure, " Tour in Greece," vol. i., p 233, *et sqq.*; and Ulrichs, " Reisen in Griechenland," p. 163, *et sqq.*

plied from the Pentelic quarries. It is of a brilliant white colour, hard, and of a fine grain.

To the left of the vast quarries which the labours of successive generations excavated in the bowels of Mount Pentelicus, may be seen a considerable shaft or gallery

THE GROTTOES OF PENTELICUS.

leading to a series of deep caverns. This entrance-hall, or natural pronaos, is finely embellished with pilasters and columns formed by constantly-accreting stalactites; and so dazzling is their whiteness that an unexperienced eye might well mistake them for alabaster. In one of he caverns approached by this sumptuous corridor lie the ruins of a chapel.

The road leading to the quarries of Pentelicus exhibit, on the very marble out of which it has been excavated, the wheel-marks of the ancient cars ; nor did they cease to bear away the precious material intended for the embellishment of Athens up to as late a date as the reign of Hadrian. At various points the blocks of marble have assumed the golden tint of the Parthenon and the Theseion. On one of these blocks stands a small dilapilated hovel, which probably served as the retreat of some devout anchorite in the early days of Christianity. It can be reached only with a long ladder.

THE GROTTO OF PANAGLIA, OR THE AGLAURIUM.

The sanctuary of Aglauros, one of the three daughters of Cecrops, was a cavern situated in the northern precipices of the Acropolis.

Aglauros is the heroine of three Attic legends of very different character. According to one, which Pausanias and Hygienus relate, she and her sisters received from Athena a chest containing Erichthonius, with strict injunctions not to open it. But Aglauros and Herse were unable to control their curiosity. They disobeyed Athena's orders, and, seized with madness at the sight of Erichthonius, flung themselves from the summit of the Acropolis.

Ovid, on the other hand, relates that the two sisters survived their act of disobedience. But Hermes afterwards visiting Athens, fell in love with Herse ; whereupon Aglauros, being filled with jealous anger through

Athena's influence, endeavoured to prevent the god from entering her sister's house. Hermes, indignant at her presumption, changed her into a stone.*

The third legend, which will be found in Plutarch and others, relates that while Athens was at one time waging a dubious and protracted war, an oracle predicted it would be victorious if some Athenian would sacrifice himself for his country's good. Thereupon Aglauros accepted the mission, and flung herself down from the Acropolis.

One of the Attic δῆμοι, or districts, was named after this patriotic heroine; and the Athenians celebrated a solemn festival and mysteries in her honour every year. And in remembrance of her self-sacrifice the Athenian ephebi, when receiving their first suit of armour, were accustomed to take an oath in the Aglaurium that they would defend their country to the last.

The exact site of the Aglaurium is now a matter of dispute. We read in Pausanias that the cavern so-called was situated at the steepest part of the Acropolis; and from a passage in the *Ion* of Euripides we know that it was near the cave of Pan, and in front of the Parthenon and Erechtheium :—

> " ὦ Πανὸς θακήματα καὶ
> παραυλίζουσα πέτρα ·
> μυχώδεσι μακραῖς,
> ἵνα χοροὺς στείβουσι ποδοῖν
> Ἀγραύλου κόραι τρίγονοι
> στάδια χλοερὰ πρὸ Παλλάδος ναῶν." †

Now, at the distance of about sixty yards from the cave of Pan, and at the foot of the precipice, may be seen

---

* Ovid, "Metamorphoses," ii. 710.
† Euripides, "Ion," ll. 506–511.

a remarkable cavern; and forty yards further, in the
same direction, another but smaller one, immediately below the citadel, and only a few yards from the northern
portico of the Erechtheium. From a stratagem adopted
by Peisistratus, when contending for the sovereignty of
Athens, it is inferred that this smaller cave was the

GROTTO OF PANAGLIA.

Aglaurium. Peisistratus, having taken possession of the
citadel, next addressed himself to the task of disarming
the Athenians. For this purpose he summoned them to
assemble in the Ænaceium, which lay to the west of the
Aglaurium. While he was haranguing them, they laid
down their arms, which were seized by the partisans of

Peisistratus, and carried into the Aglaurium, undoubtedly
that they might thence be transferred to the citadel
itself.

Now an ancient flight of stairs has been discovered
near the Erechtheium, which communicates with the
smaller of the two caverns, and, consequently, if the latter
were the Aglaurium, would render easy the stratagem of
Peisistratus and his faction.

This flight leads into the cavern, and from the cavern
passes through a deep gap in the rock, and opens out in
the face of the cliff a little below the foundation. Though
now choked up, it was practicable as late as 1844.

We may conclude, therefore, that the cave to which
we have referred was the Aglaurium, and that the access
to it from the Acropolis was in the immediate vicinity of
the northern façade of the Erechtheium. Leake, indeed,
is of opinion that the Aglaurium, which was no temple,
but simply a sacred enclosure, comprised both the larger
and smaller cavern, the former being more particularly
dedicated to Herse and the latter to Aglauros. With all
due deference, we submit that there is no foundation for
such a conjecture in any of the Greek writers.

It should be noted that, according to Herodotus, the
Persians, when beleaguering Athens, obtained entrance into
the Acropolis through or near the sanctuary of Aglauros;
and Bishop Wordsworth is probably correct in supposing
that they discovered, and made use of, the secret staircase
in the smaller cavern.*

* Wordsworth, "Athens and Attica," pp 86, 87.

IV

Ancient Rome.

THE CATACOMBS OF ROME.

THE celebrated Roman Catacombs are undoubtedly one of the most remarkable remains of that Roman civilization which has bequeathed to us the vestiges of so many wonders.

These catacombs form a series of interminable subterranean galleries, extending underneath the city itself, and in the adjacent country, and containing no less, it is supposed, than six millions of tombs.

But before we trace their history, or describe their present condition, it will be advisable, perhaps, that we should supply the reader with a few details in illustration of the antiquity and universality of this mode of sculpture.

From the earliest ages a great number of civilized peoples, as well as of others who were less advanced,—Egyptians, Hebrews, Persians, Greeks, Hindus, Guanchos, Scythians,—have all, like the Romans, resorted to the religious practice of interring their dead; with this exception, that some deposited them simply in the earth, while others, after having embalmed them, preserved

them in their own houses, or in caverns, natural or artificial.

No other mode of interment, says a French writer,* was
practised in Syria. Wherever the Tyrians penetrated, to
Malta, Sicily, Sardinia, similar burial-places have been
discovered. Beulé has ascertained the existence of catacombs at Carthage; Renan has seen them in Phoenicia;
Asia Minor, the Cyrenaïc, and the Chersonesus contain a
great number. It is the same among the Etruscans, to
whom we are accustomed to attribute a national origin.

The Jews,† the Phoenicians, the worshippers of Mithra
and Sabazius, sometimes the pagans themselves, buried
their dead underground. The custom of cremation, or
burning the dead, gradually fell into disuse at Rome from
the epoch of the Antonines, and seems to have become
almost obsolete in the time of Macrobius. So that the
Christians eventually did not monopolize this mode of
interment at Rome. In the third century it was very
generally adopted.

Here, however, we must make a distinction: the ancient
Romans, as well pagans as Jews or Christians, who in-
humed their dead, deposited them either in *hypogea* or
crypts,—private vaults, so to speak, which at the most
contained the remains of only a few families; or in *catacombs*,—common places of burial, where, after death, were
brought together a great host of persons who had lived
in the same faith, or simply at the same epoch.

The hypogea and crypts are the more ancient; as for

* M. Boisselier, in a very interesting article on " Les Catacombes de Rome,"
in the *Revue des Deux Mondes*, 5th September 1865.

† Up to the present date, two Jewish catacombs have been discovered at
Rome ; that of the Transtevère, which is anterior to Christianity, and that of
the Via Appia. As for heathen hypogea, they begin to be tolerably common.

the catacombs (at Rome), they do not seem to date further back than the last days of paganism.

The word *catacombs* itself has no very explicit signification : it is derived from the Greek words κατά, "below" or "near to," and κύμβος, "a cavity." Some authorities, however, trace it to κατά and τύμβος, a "tomb," and assert that it was formerly spelt *catatombs*, not *catacombs*. The latter form, however, has become so incorporated in the language, that it would be useless, as well as pedantic, to attempt any alteration.

However this may be, the name was first specially consecrated, according to St. Gregory, to designate the excavation in which the sacred bodies of St. Peter and St. Paul had been deposited ; and it was not until somewhat later that it was applied to all the subterranean galleries which were converted into public cemeteries. It has even been asserted that the early Christian writers never applied the word *catacomb* to the burial-places of the great city, but only to a chapel of St. Sebastian, in which, according to an ancient Roman calendar, the bodies of Paul and Peter were enshrined, during the consulship of Tuscus and Bassus, in 258. In ancient documents, instead of "catacombs," we meet with the words "crypts" or "cemeteries."

The opinion most generally accepted down to our days was, that the catacombs of Rome ought to be looked upon as old and abandoned quarries,—the asylum of vagabonds, the refuge of assassins,—whither the early Christians were guided by their slaves, and where they assembled together for the purpose of worshipping God in their own fashion; and afterwards, for the sake of living in happy communion, apart from the luxuries and vices of a hateful world. Many people placed no confidence in the discoveries of Bosio, Bottari, and other men of science, but ridiculed as a religious prejudice the opinion of those who looked upon the catacombs as the tombs of Christian martyrs.

It is very certain that in the fierce days of persecution, under Nero and Domitian, Trajan, Hadrian, and Severus, the Christians took refuge in the catacombs, and there celebrated in secrecy the ceremonies of their religion ; but the recent discoveries of Marchi and Rossi have made it not less certain that the catacombs also served them as a place of sepulture; and more, that, despite the contrary opinion which prevailed for upwards of two centuries, these catacombs are not, for the most part, deserted quarries, but were entirely and completely excavated by the Christians.

The power of the spirit of association, when placed at the service of a new faith, is sufficient, in addition to the well-known reverence paid by the early Christians to the resting-places of their dead, to explain how a poor and proscribed community could accomplish so great a work ; especially as it is now considered very probable that among their proselytes they included many wealthy personages.

It should be added that, at the epoch when the Christians began their excavations, the Jews, and the worshippers of Mithra and Sabazius, had already been at work on Roman soil for a similar purpose ; and as the latter met with no opposition from the authorities, it is very probable that the Christians were also unimpeded. We may confidently affirm that in the beginning, at all vents, and for nearly two centuries, they were under no necessity of concealing their works.

Originally, the cemeteries of Rome were private tombs onstructed by opulent Christians for themselves and their brethren, and whose proprietorship they retained under he safeguard of the law.

But with the times the circumstances changed. At he close of the second century, references occur in eccle- iastical writers to cemeteries not belonging to private ndividuals, but openly acknowledged as the property of he Church. Such was the one the superintendence of vhich Pope Zephyrinus confided to Calixtus. Some years ater, under Pope Fabian, there were already several cata- :ombs ; and their number continued to increase up to the ·eign of Constantine.

It is probable that the Christian community, to shelter tself from the Roman law, which persecuted severely all ecret societies, and allowed no corporations to acquire and nold property without examination, formed itself into an ssociation authorized by the imperial decree, after the nanner of the *collegia funeratricia* (or "funeral societies") hen so numerous at Rome, which were sanctioned by uthority, and consisted of poor people paying a small um at regular intervals so as to provide for their decent nterment after death. At all events, as Boisselier remarks, f the Christians did not comply with the same formali- ies as these legalized associations, it is certain that they not the less derived a very great advantage from their xistence.

The history of the catacombs is more difficult to trace,

however, than their origin, especially if we endeavour to follow it up to the primitive epoch.

For the first two centuries there is an absolute want of all documentary evidence. Until we arrive at the reign of Decius, we are compelled to trust entirely to conjectures.

During this considerable period the Christians seem to have enjoyed nearly always a certain degree of liberty. It is true that at the outset their doctrines were not taught without danger and difficulty; but the persecutions of Nero and Domitian, notwithstanding their fierceness, were only passing storms, and it is not certain that they extended to the catacombs: in the interval, under Vespasian and Titus, the disciples of Christ were not oppressed by the secular arm. The emperors who succeeded, down to Septimius Severus, adopted against them various administrative measures, which were sometimes carried into rigorous execution, but from which the Christians generally contrived to escape,—and which, at all events, did not arrest the triumphant progress of the religion of the Cross.

Under Caracalla, under Alexander Severus, under the two Philips, the Christians were not only not persecuted, but they were protected. And, finally, down to the reign of Decius, even when the Christian community was oppressed, its cemeteries were respected. Neither from history nor tradition do we learn that any attempt had been made to despoil them. We read nothing of any measures of this kind either in the Lives of the Saints, the Acts of the Martyrs, the celebrated Letter of Pliny, or Trajan's not less celebrated reply.

The persecution of the dead dates from the reign of Decius, and commenced in Africa.

During the rule of Hilarianus, says Tertullian, the people began to cry that they would have no more cemeteries! And, in the madness of their Bacchanalian excesses, they dared to drag the bodies of the Christians from the repose of the sepulchre and the asylum of death.

The example proved contagious. In 257, the Emperor Valerianus prohibited the faithful from entering their catacombs; and when Pope Sextus II. infringed the imperial decree, he was beheaded, with his deacons and priests, in the catacombs of St. Praetextatus. The Emperor Galienus revoked the orders of his predecessors, but the impulse had been given; the Christian cemeteries did not recover the immunity which they had previously enjoyed. From thenceforth, down to the reign of Constantine, tradition speaks only of martyrs put to death in the catacombs; as, for instance, of the Emperor Diocletian burying alive, in the catacombs of the Via Salaria, a numerous company of Christians who frequented them in spite of the imperial edicts.

With Constantine, a change came over the spirit of the scene. The catacombs were repaired, enlarged, embellished; magnificent entrances and convenient staircases constructed; in fine, the ancient asylum of those who suffered for the truth's sake was honoured in every possible manner. But in seeking to beautify and dignify the catacombs, the enthusiasts greatly injured their character, and destroyed many of their associations.

After a while, the primitive faith grew colder as it grew victorious; and in proportion as its earnestness diminished, so did the reverence diminish which the subterranean cemeteries had formerly inspired. From the reign of Constans, inhumations in the catacombs became much rarer. Then, after a brief period of indecision, the custom of interring the dead in churches came into vogue, and the catacombs were finally abandoned. For just five hundred years they had been used as places of sepulture.

Men continued, however, for a long time to visit the catacombs, in remembrance of the era of persecution, and to do homage to the relics of the martyrs. St. Jerome relates that, when a child, he descended into them on the Lord's Day, with his companions, and penetrated into the very crypts, whose walls, on every side, revealed long rows of dead bodies, and where an obscurity so profound prevailed that one was tempted to look upon the scene as realizing the words of the prophet: "Living, they descended into hell." Pilgrims came to them from every country in Christendom, as is evident from the curious ancient notices and inscriptions which now guide the stranger to the tombs of the martyrs. Some itineraries of pilgrims who visited them in the last years of the Empire are also extant. All who came to see them desired to carry away some memorials of their pilgrimage. Generally they poured out a profuse quantity of precious perfumes on the shattered stones of the tomb, and carefully collected the smallest drops which escaped through the lower crevices, after having touched the body of the saint. We read of a queen of Lombardy who sent a priest expressly to collect and bring away the oil of the lamps that burned near the tomb of the martyrs.

This *cultus* was interrupted by the invasions of the barbarians. To protect the holy relics from the ravages of Alaric, Vitigès, and Ataulf, they were removed from the martyrs' tombs and distributed among the different churches of Rome. Thenceforth no reason for visiting the catacombs existed ; all traces and recollection of them were gradually lost; no person felt any interest in them.

Yet the inscriptions found in the catacombs prove, by the very date which is affixed to them, that some few persons, at different epochs, were emboldened by curiosity to risk themselves in their galleries, and explore some of their recesses. Thus, an inscription traced with charcoal in a chamber of the cemetery of St. Praetextatus, and recorded by Marangoni, bears the date of 1490, and is thus conceived :—

HIC D. RAYNUTIUS DE FARNESIO FUIT CUM SODALIBUS.

(D. R. de Farnese came here with his friends.) Another inscription, traced in an adjacent chamber, is dated 1467, and bears the names of an abbé of S. Hermèes of Pisa ($\overline{Dns}$ abb id est $\overline{Dns}$ $\overline{sci}$ Ermetis), and of eight of his monks.

But these visits were wholly exceptional, and we may say, with the Abbé Martigny,* that, up to the epoch of Bosio, the sacred hypogea of the early Christians and martyrs were almost completely forgotten. The Christopher Columbus of these sacred crypts, says Martigny, somewhat affectedly, is the immortal Bosio.

Nevertheless, certain learned and studious pioneers had prepared the way for Bosio. For Panvinio, towards the middle of the sixteenth century, drew up a list, taking as his guides some ancient books, of forty-three Roman cemeteries. And in 1578, the Dominican Alphonso

* "Dictionnaire des Antiquités Chrétiennes," sub nom. "Catacombes."

Ciacconio descended into the cemetery of Priscilla, under the Via Salaria, explored it carefully, and collected in an album a variety of sketches which he had taken.

About the same time, Philippe Wingh, a gentleman of Louvain, and nephew of the antiquary, Philippe Wingh, having visited Rome, formed a friendship with Ciacconio, visited in his turn the cemetery of Priscilla, where he deciphered a great number of inscriptions, and made many drawings, which were unfortunately lost.

Bosio appears to have had the assistance both of the drawings of Wingh and the " Itinerary" of Panvinio. We may, therefore, suppose that he was set on the track of the catacombs by the discovery of that of St. Priscilla.

Antonio Bosio, says the Abbé Martigny, was a Maltese by birth, an advocate by profession, and resided at Rome, towards the middle of the sixteenth century, in the capacity of an agent of the order of Malta. Never was there antiquarian more enthusiastic or persevering than he. This man of genius, whose physical strength equalled his moral energy, consecrated thirty-five years of his life, and considerable sums of money, to exploring the catacombs in all directions.

Assisted by the documents which he had in his hands, he set himself, at first, to seek the site where, according to the most plausible probabilities, each cemetery would be found. He seized with promptitude, and worked out with the rarest sagacity, every sign which accidentally presented itself,—such as a subsidence of the soil, the excavation of a well or cellar; and when any access opened up to his persevering researches, there was no danger nor obstacle which could prevent him from venturing into the catacombs. He was compelled more than once, with his own hands, and at the peril of his life, to force an entrance into galleries which had long been closed up by alluvial drift or ancient landslips. He himself relates that, wishing to visit with some security the cemetery of St. Calixtus, he provided himself with a clew of thread, one end of which he attached to the entrance. Then with spades and pickaxes, and an abundant supply of torches and provisions, he plunged into these immense labyrinths, not to emerge from them until after many days and nights of incessant explorations. He allowed nothing of any interest to escape him; he copied all the inscriptions; brought to light every painting; and made his plans and tracings with a faithfulness which our modern savants, including Agincourt and the Père Marchi, have fully acknowledged.

Bosio died before he was able to publish the result of his researches. His manuscript was not printed until thirty years after his death, when it appeared in a large folio volume entitled *Roma Sotterranea*, edited by the oratorist Giovanni Severano. The first Roman edition is dated 1632; fifteen years later, Aringhi published an edition in Latin; this is the best known.

Since the days of Bosio, subterranean Rome has been explored in all directions, and some important works have been devoted to it. In the first rank of these we must place the labours of Aringhi, Boldetti, Bottari, Marchi, and, more recently, of M. de Rossi, who has undertaken a gigantic work from a new point of view, and completely demolishes the erroneous notions of the catacombs which, unfortunately, have been so long prevalent.* Thanks to the labours of these men of science,

* "Roma Sotterranea Christiana ed illustrata dal cav. J. B. de Rossi," tome I. (Rome, 1864).

the precious monuments of the origin of Christianity have become imperishable, and are for ever placed within reach of the student. Unhappily, the subterranean galleries are daily more and more obstructed by frequent landslips, and stand in urgent need of a system of reparation and support which the poverty or indifference of the Roman government foolishly refuses.

The Roman catacombs enjoy a kind of legendary renown, which several tragic adventures, occurring at different dates, have not a little contributed to support. Independent visitors, wandering in the labyrinths of these sepulchral galleries, have lost their way, and perished of hunger. The best known of these accidents, which, however, had no fatal issue, occurred to the French artist Robert,* and has furnished Delille with the subject of a remarkable episode in his poem " On the Imagination."

As this poem, notwithstanding its many merits, is almost unknown to English readers, we shall quote a portion of the original French, and afterwards supply a translation of the entire episode :—

"Sous les remparts de Rome et sous ses vastes plaines
Sont des antres profonds, des voûtes souterraines,
Qui, pendant deux mille ans, creusés par les humains,
Donnèrent leurs rochers aux palais des Romains ;
Avec ses rois, ses dieux et sa magnificence,
Rome entière sortit de cet abîme immense.
Depuis, loin des regards et du fer des tyrans,
L'Eglise encore naissante y cacha ses enfants,
Jusqu'au jour où du sein de cette nuit profonde,
Triomphante, elle vint donner des lois au monde,
Et marqua de sa croix les drapeaux des Césars.
Jaloux de tout connaître, un jeune amant des arts,
L'amour de ses parents, l'espoir de la peinture,
Brûlait de visiter cette demeure obscure,
De notre antique foi vénérable berceau.
Un fil dans une main et dans l'autre un flambeau,

* The Louvre at Paris possesses several pictures by Hubert (Robert', representing ancient ruins contrasted with the common scenes of modern life.

Il entre, il se confie à ces voûtes nombreuses,
Qui croisent en tous sens leurs routes ténébreuses ;
Il aime à voir ce lieu, sa triste majesté,
Ce palais de la nuit, cette sombre cité,
Ces temples où le Christ vit ses premiers fidèles,
Et de ces grands tombeaux les ombres éternelles.
Dans un coin écarté se présente un réduit,
Mystérieux asile où l'espoir le conduit.
Il voit des vases saints et des urnes pieuses,
Des vierges, des martyrs dépouilles précieuses ;
Il saisit ce trésor, il veut poursuivre, hélas !
Il a perdu le fil qui conduisait ses pas ;
Il cherche, mais en vain, il s'égare, il se trouble,
Il s'éloigne, il revient, et sa crainte redouble ;
Il prend tous les chemins que lui montre la peur ;
Enfin, de route en route et d'erreur en erreur,
Dans les enfoncements de cette obscure enceinte,
Il trouve un vaste espace, effrayant labyrinthe,
D'où vingt chemins divers conduisent à l'entour.
Lequel choisir ? Lequel doit le conduire au jour ?
Il les consulte tous, il les prend, il les quitte ;
Il appelle, l'écho redouble sa frayeur ;
De sinistres pensers viennent glacer son cœur.
L'astre heureux qu'il regrette a mesuré dix heures
Depuis qu'il est errant dans ces noires demeures ;
Ce lieu d'effroi, ce lieu d'un silence éternel,
En trois lustres entiers voit à peine un mortel ;
Et, pour comble d'effroi, dans cette nuit funeste,
Du flambeau qui le guide il voit périr le reste.
Craignant que chaque pas, que chaque mouvement,
En agitant la flamme, en use l'aliment,
Quelquefois il s'arrête et demeure immobile.
Vaines précautions ! tout soin est inutile,
L'heure approche, et déjà son cœur épouvanté
Croit de l'affreuse nuit sentir l'obscurité."

Imitated.

Beneath the walls of Rome, beneath its plains,
Lie antres deep, and subterranean vaults,
Which, for two thousand years by human toil
Hewn out, supplied their rocks to raise aloft
The Roman palaces. Yes ; with its kings,
Its gods, and all its splendour, Rome arose
From this immense abyss. In later times,
Remote from tyrants' wrath and cruel eyes,
The still-young Church her children here concealed,
Until the day when, from the deep obscure
Emerging glorious, she gave her laws
To the wide world, and on the Cæsars' flag
Her cross inscribed.
　　　　　　　On knowledge all intent,
Once a young artist much desired to seek

The depths of this mysterious abode,
The venerable cradle of our faith.
A clew in one hand, and in one a torch,
He enters; boldly trusts his brave young life
To these unnumbered vaults which wind and cross
And intercross in a perplexing maze.
O'erjoyed he looks around : how gloomy grand
This palace of the night, this sombre city,
These temples where Christ blessed his earliest saints
These mighty tombs with their eternal shades !

Now in a far recess a nook he sees,
Asylum strange ! Thither he bends his steps,
And lo, before him sacred urns are piled,
And holy vessels, treasuring up the dust,
The precious dust of virgins, martyrs, saints !
Shall not this wealth be his?
                              And now he fain
His winding way would trace to its departure.
Alas, the clew is lost ! He seeks—in vain !
This way and that; he goes, he comes—in vain !
Dismay strikes to his heart, and every path
He tries in turn which panic fear suggests.
At length, from route to route haphazard straying,
Deep in the heart of this dim lower world
He finds a mighty labyrinthine space
Where twenty roads converge.   Which shall he choose?
Which will conduct him to the wished-for day?
First one he tries, and then he tries a second;
A third, a fourth ; he calls aloud, his fears
Redoubled by the echoes of his cries.
Ah, what dread thoughts crowd fast upon his brain !
Ten hours the sun has measured since he plunged,
Unwise, into these awful shades, this haunt
Of solitude and silence, seldom trod
By foot of man; and now, to fill his cup
Of bitterness, the torch which lights his path
Fast wavers to its end ! Each step he dreads,
Each movement, lest it quench the trembling flame.
Sometimes he halts, and stands immovable :
Precaution vain ! and fruitless every care !
The hour wears on, and even now his heart
Shrinks from the darkness of the coming night!

But here we may terminate both our quotation and
our paraphrase, lest we should weary the reader. It is
enough to say that at last the wanderer finds his missing
thread, and begins to retrace his steps. His long absence
meanwhile has alarmed his friends, who have entered the

catacombs in search of him, and arrive in time to refresh and assist him when fainting with fatigue, and worn with hunger and alarm.

A somewhat similar story, but differing in many of its details, is told by Mr. Macfarlane.*

In the year 1798, soon after the first entrance into Rome of the French Republican army, under General Berthier, a gay company of young officers resolved on an excursion to the catacombs. With characteristic irreverence, they converted their visit into a revel, and carried with them an abundant supply of provisions, wine, and brandy.

After sauntering through one or two of the galleries, and jesting at the sacred expressions which covered their walls, they sat themselves down in one of the oratories or little chapels, and caroused until their liquor was exhausted, and each brain on fire.

Then they resumed their exploration of the crypts, descending into the lowest tier, and betting with one another who would venture furthest into their labyrinthine recesses. One among them was not less celebrated for his impiety than for his reckless daring. He refused to leave the crypts until he had visited all; and darting away, a torch in his hand, but unaccompanied by any guide, he plunged into a lateral gallery. Heedless of what he was doing, he moved forward, and still forward; from one crypt he turned into another; until, at length, his torch burning low, and his intoxication evaporating, he began to retrace his steps. With considerable difficulty he found his way back to the chapel where he and his comrades had held their profane festivities and sang

* C. Macfarlane, "The Catacombs of Rome," pp. 87–100.

aloud their blasphemous songs.   It was deserted.   As he made this appalling discovery, his torch flickered, and he was only just in time to light a second, which he fortunately had with him.

After weary wanderings, he found the steps leading to the second tier of crypts; but his companions were not there.   He shouted their names aloud, and besought them to desist from further trickery; for he thought they had hidden themselves in some nook or corridor.   There was no reply,—except the echoes of his own voice. Completely sobered by his alarm, he found his way to the upper crypt, and hastened with all possible speed to the entrance of the catacomb.   The gates were closed. He shouted; with the fragment of a tombstone, he beat furiously against the railings; he became frantic, and filled the air with his shrieks.   But it was night, and the place was wholly deserted.

His mental agony, and the dry dusty air of the catacombs, had parched the very roof of his mouth, and he suffered terribly from thirst.   His torch, too, had burned down to the end.   In this extremity he gathered up some remains of torches which his friends had left behind them, and lighted them successively, as one after the other grew extinct.   While the last was rapidly blazing away, he bethought him of retracing his steps to the oratory where he and his comrades had held their revel; but as he stumbled along, his foot slipped; he fell, and his torch being extinguished, he found himself in total darkness.   As he groped his way, he fell through a chasm.   The fall was slight, for the chamber beneath was very full; but as he alighted among crackling, clattering, and crumbling bones, his nerves sustained another shock, and he could scarcely maintain his self-control.

However, with an effort he released himself from his horrible position, regained the crypt above, and on his hands and knees crept slowly onward until he reached the oratory. Here a *foramen*, or opening, admitted both air and moonlight; and seating himself on the floor, with the moon's beams pouring brilliantly upon him, he endeavoured to compose his excited brain. He recalled the sayings of the French sceptics, of Voltaire and D'Alembert, and argued that a fear of death or the dead was unworthy of an enlightened mind. But with his atheistic recollections came back the memories of childish superstitions, and he trembled with terror. He could have marched undaunted on a gleaming line of bayonets; but to pass a night in a charnel-house was too severe a trial.

His thirst grew intolerable. Looking about, he caught sight of a bottle glittering in the moonlight, near the stone altar. The wanderer seized it, and drank eagerly of its contents. Instead of water it was filled with brandy, and in a few minutes, the potion acting with violence on a frame already burning with thirst and fever, he became delirious. Wild visions swept before him; dark spectres seemed to gather round him; the skulls lying on either hand seemed reanimated with ghastly eyes that penetrated to his very soul; the bones of the dead became instinct with life; they rose, and clattered, and loud shrieks escaped from fleshless lips: it was a phantasmagoria of terror, in which the occasional sounds that reached him from without, and the flickering beams of the moonlight, became the agents of ever-new delusions.

It is impossible to doubt that death must have been the

issue of this fearful experience, had not the morning
brought with it some fresh visitors to the catacombs,
who discovered the young officer in a state of stupor, and
removed him to the military hospital.   There he lay for
many months, suffering from a brain-fever of the worst
kind, and from its consequent exhaustion.   When he
recovered, he was found to be an altered man.   That
night in the catacombs had cured him of his sceptical
indifference.   He had been taught the weakness of man
in the valley of the shadow of death unless he is supported by a Divine Hand.   So he abandoned his Voltaire,
his Diderot, his D'Alembert, and devoted himself to a
patient and humble study of Christ's gospel,—finding in
its pages a joy and a consolation of which his erring
spirit had previously had no conception.   As a Christian
he lived, and as a Christian he died.

It should be added that he had been purposely shut
up in the catacombs by his brother-officers, who thought
in this way to punish him for his extravagant boasting.
Themselves inflamed with wine and brandy, they were
unable to apprehend the evil consequences that might
ensue from a jest of so serious a character.   It is probable
that the guides did not miss him out of so large a company;
or, if they did, were not unwilling to join in administer-
ing a severe lesson to a fool-hardy Frenchman.

We now proceed to a brief description of the catacombs.
Let the reader figure to himself a long series of interminable galleries, from three feet and a quarter to five
feet in width, and from three to fourteen feet in height,
intersecting each other continually, so as to form a
multitude of cross-roads, and constitute an inextricable

labyrinth. There is no masonry, however; neither pillar nor roof; they are excavated out of the earth, which is firm and hard enough to support itself. The walls of these subterranean streets are formed by the niches, or *loculi*, in which the dead bodies are placed. At intervals, we meet with broader spaces, generally square, which are called *chambers*, or *cubicula*. Through shafts, or openings, placed at distances of three hundred feet, the outer air is admitted; but many of them are choked up with crumbling soil. Nearly all the galleries are excavated in two or more stories, which communicate with one another by means of stairs.

We have asserted that if the primitive Christians preferred the subterranean cemeteries, it was less to escape from the watchfulness of despotic power than to remain faithful to the traditions of the early Church, —which, on emerging, as it were, from the Jewish community, had preserved this Jewish custom. Let us add that it may also have been designed as an imitation of the tomb of Christ, who, in death as in life, was necessarily the Exemplar of every devout Christian. It is not to be doubted, says Boisselier, that the sepulchre of Joseph of Arimathea, of which use had never been made, and which had been cut out of the solid rock, with its horizontal niche, surrounded by the single and simple ornament of an *arcosolium*, was adopted as the model of the first Christian tombs.

At the outset, when the dead were grouped around the martyrs and bishops of the Church, the catacombs were of limited extent; it was not until the reigns of Caracalla, Alexander Severus, and the two Philips, when the Christian community was undisturbed by persecution,

that they acquired the immense proportions which astonish the modern explorer.

It is easy to understand how they were gradually
developed : in the galleries first constructed, the niches
in which the dead found a resting-place were wide, and
at some distance from one another ; a great deal of room
was lost. But the number of the faithful increasing, it
became necessary to contract the dimensions of the tombs,
to set them more closely together, and to fill up the empty
intervals. But even this expedient did not long prove
sufficient, and it was decided to enlarge the catacombs.
They were excavated on different levels ; as many as five
tiers of galleries were sometimes superimposed in the
same crypt. The uppermost was twenty-one to twenty-
eight feet below the surface ; the last attained a depth of
three hundred. These enlargements provided an ample
space, and for generations the Christians remained contented ; however, the Church continually increasing its
numbers, the ramifications of the catacombs were so
extended as at many points to unite, and by uniting to
form a cemetery. The cemeteries, therefore, are simply
the reunion of some of these originally isolated crypts ;
and the reason they possess so great a number of entrances is, that each crypt had its own, which was never
shut up. All the cemeteries would probably have been
linked together in time, so as to compose one immense
subterranean city of the dead, had they not in several
cases been separated by deep and marshy hollows, which
in stormy weather expanded into lakes.

Down to this epoch, all the works were freely and
openly executed ; no need existed to disguise the entrances ; the magnificent flights of steps opened out into

the fields. But when the fierce winds of persecution swept destructively over the suffering Church,—that is, from the reign of Decius down to that of Constantine,— the Christians were compelled to resort to stratagem and secrecy. The narrow and sinuous staircases were approached through deserted quarries; the earth excavated from the new galleries was piled up in the disused chambers, where it may be seen to this very day; the crypts were obstructed; the passages were concealed; and the bodies of the martyrs were so jealously hidden from every curious eye, that many of them eventually could not be recovered. These precautionary measures were adopted down to the epoch of Constantine.

Under the sway of the first Christian emperor, the fanatical devotion of the faithful involved the catacombs in a new danger. Every one wished to be interred as near as possible to the martyrs. When a niche was selected, it was made at the cost of some former occupant. Unhappily, a large number of the ancient inscriptions were destroyed without scruple, and niches excavated in walls which were covered with admirable frescoes. It is needless to point out the greatness of the loss the Church has sustained by this wholesale destruction. As historical evidences, these inscriptions and frescoes would probably have been of priceless value.

Yet another misfortune. The tombs, formerly constructed by the Christians themselves as a high and holy work, were thenceforth excavated by a hired company of mercenaries, who speculated both in the ground and the amount of labour to be bestowed upon it. You may still see on the walls of the catacombs the traces of " contracts " and " agreements " signed by this harpy brood of speculators, the forerunners of our modern undertakers, and equally ready to make a trade of death.

Soon afterwards, when the tide of barbarian invasion rolled up to the walls of Rome, the catacombs were abandoned; and with so much precipitation, that you will find many chambers and galleries prepared by the excavator which were never occupied.

A considerable proportion of the inscriptions and artistic embellishments of the crypts belong to the reign of Constantine, or to the period of his immediate successors, when they were regarded as a *terra sancta ;* and popes and kings, prelates and princes, were rendered happy in their last moments by the reflection that they should sleep in the company of the holy martyrs. The artificial distinctions of rank were levelled before this all-engrossing sentiment, and the proudest sovereign of Europe thought himself honoured by a resting-place beside some poor and obscure Christian, some hewer of wood or drawer of water, on whom, in life, he would not have deigned to look. The following are a few of the names* of the great and powerful who

> " So ensepulchred in pomp do lie,
> That kings for such a grave might wish to die."

Anaclitus, fifth Pope or Bishop of Rome.

Pope Gregory the Great,—he who despatched St. Augustine on the mission of converting England to the Christian faith.

Popes Gregory II. and III.

Pope Leo IX. (died 1055, the last Pope interred in the catacombs).

The Emperor Honorius.

The Emperor Valentinian.

The Emperor Otho II.

Ceadwalla, the famous hero of the West Saxons.

Offa, a Mercian king.

* Gaume, " Les Trois Romes," iv. 39

Ina, King of the Angles; with Queen Eldeburga, his wife.

Mary, wife of the Emperor Honorius, and daughter of his great general, Stilicho.

The Empress Agnes, a woman of saintly character.

Charlotte, the unhappy Queen of Cyprus.

Matilda, Countess of Tuscany, the friend of Pope Gregory VII., and the wealthy benefactress of the Apostolic See, to which, by formal instruments, she bequeathed her vast inheritance.*

How great a misfortune it was felt to be excluded from a place in the catacombs, we can guess from an inscription discovered in a crypt under the Appian Way :—

"O tempora infausta, quibus inter sacra et vota, ne in cavernis quidem salvari possumus! Quid miserius vitâ? Sed quid miserius in morte, cum ab amicis et parentibus sepeliri nequeant!"

That is: O wretched times, when we are unable to find a refuge in caverns, amongst sacrifices and prayers! What can be more miserable than life? But what more miserable than death, since we may not be laid at rest among our friends and kinsmen!

The irruptions of the barbarians were not only fatal to the art treasures of the Imperial City, to her arches and columns and temples, her palaces and churches, but even to her vast underground cemeteries, which were pillaged successively by Goth and Hun in quest of hidden wealth. Next came the avaricious Lombards, and these were followed by the Saracens; until the Christian no longer dared to bury his dead in their crypts, or worship in their chapels.   From the eleventh to the fourteenth century Rome was distracted by the feuds of her jealous patricians, —her Orsinis, Colonnas, Savellis, Frangipanis; and the catacombs became the resort of desperate conspirators and armed insurgents, or offered a temporary refuge to the timorous and oppressed.   We are told that Cola di Rienzi, in the last hour of his romantic career, was advised

* Dean Milman, "Latin Christianity," iv. 204.

by a friend to fly for safety to the underground Rome; but that, like Nero, he replied, he would not bury himself alive. The story is very doubtful; but it illustrates the uses to which the catacombs were at that time degraded. A further and more significant illustration may be borrowed from Petrarch :—

> " Quasi spelunca di ladron son fatti,
> Tal, ch' à buon solamente uscio si chiude ;
> E tra le altari, e tra le statue ignude,
> Ogni impresa crudel par che si tratti."

> Like robbers' caves they are become, to which
> Only the good admission are denied ;
> And among sacred shrines and statues saintly
> Nefarious projects are in secret hatched.

And so the work of destruction and spoliation went on. The galleries were choked with rubbish, the entrances closed, the flights of steps broken, the inscriptions defaced, the statues and altars were cruelly and thoughtlessly demolished. The ploughshare of havoc was driven through subterranean Rome.

It was about 1535—or, at all events, in the pontificate of Paul III.—that attempts were first made to repair these ravages, and that some of the more remarkable crypts were cleared and lighted. A few years later, and the great restorer of the underground city arose; Father Antonio Bosio, who occupied himself from 1567 to 1600 with an incredible zeal, perseverance, and sagacity, in a thorough exploration of the catacombs, and whose researches have been the foundation on which all later explorers have wrought.

Italy contains two subterranean cities, which have been unearthed, as it were, in a very similar manner, for the edification of the modern world. From Pompeii our scholars have gained inestimable treasures of knowledge in reference to the manners and customs of antiquity; from underground Rome the Christian has gathered a valuable fund of information bearing upon the history of the primitive Church. A visit to either City of the Dead is calculated to fill the thoughtful mind with very serious impressions, but impressions of a very different character, as the Abbé Gerbet has eloquently pointed out.* "Nothing," he justly says, "can be more desolate than the aspect of Pompeii, half rising from its ashes, not to be resuscitated and repeopled, but to assume, as it were, the mask of life, to entice the balmy airs of spring and the sweet breath of nature once more to wander in those empty streets which the sun so uselessly illuminates. The deep shadows of the catacombs produce on the soul an entirely different effect from the sunshine of Pompeii; for the grand charm of these places chiefly lies in the contrast between the night and darkness which reigned around and the spiritual day which beamed upon their old inhabitants, and is still reflected from their graves." Pompeii recalls to us the nothingness and cruelty, the vanities and lusts and horrors, of the pagan world; the catacombs remind us of the purity of Christ's religion, of the new dignity with which it invested human life, of the new hopes with which it illuminated the grave. Pompeii is wholly material; subterranean Rome as completely spiritual. For we forget the mouldering bones of the saintly dead in our remembrance of their immortality; we forget the darkness of the tomb in the promise of the abundant light of Heaven. And so while Pompeii saddens and depresses the thoughtful pilgrim; subterranean Rome, that other "City of the Dead," cheers, elevates, and

* Gerbet, "Rome Chrétienne," tome premier.

inspires him. He looks around and sighs not : with Prudentius he exclaims,—

" Non mortua, sed data somno."

He knows that they are not dead, but sleeping.

To the major part of the catacombs now accessible, the entrances are to be found in the churches which, at the epoch of the triumph of Christianity over its enemies, were built above their site, and in the place of the small primitive chapels, the *cellae* or *memoriae majorum*. Such

A PRIMITIVE ENTRANCE TO THE CATACOMBS OF ROME.

is the case with those of St. Sebastian, St. Agnes, and St. Lawrence-without-the-Walls. To many other cemeteries admission is obtained in the midst of the vines which flourish over a portion of the soil of ancient Rome ; in others the entrance is completely lost, and the traveller gains admittance through the external rents or air-shafts, or through openings accidentally made in the surface of the ground.

We have no space to name the sixty and more cemetcries which are now-a-days explored, and which, in their aggregate, constitute the Catacombs of Rome; we shall speak only of the best known.

The largest, and the one which contains the greatest number of celebrated sepulchres, is the *Cemetery of Calixtus*, under the Appian Way. Ancient documents agree in asserting that from Zephyrinus to Melchiades (A.D. 202–314) all the Popes were buried there. Unfortunately they are not so unanimous in reference to the site it occupied; and its identification is entirely due to the well-directed and enthusiastic labours of the Cavaliere de Rossi.

The Crypt of Lucina is united to the vast cemetery of Calixtus, but it has its own independent history. Evidently it is one of those hypogea which belong to the earliest days of Christianity. It occupies a space one hundred feet in length by one hundred and twenty-four in breadth. Such were the dimensions of the field purchased by Lucina, in which she caused a tomb to be constructed for herself and her brothers in Christ. Above the site of this crypt may be seen the remains of an ancient monument, whose appearance and proportions, to judge from the foundations, must have been magnificent. It was, undoubtedly, one of those funereal edifices, one of those *memoriae martyrum*, which it was customary to raise *above ground* to mark the locality of the *underground* sepulchre. We may therefore conclude that the crypt of Lucina is one of those ancient catacombs which were the beginning of the great Christian cemeteries.

The cemeteries of St. Praetextatus and St. Sebastian, under the Vatican Hill, are situated close to that of

Calixtus, with which they have been frequently con-
founded. The latter has been rendered famous by the
death of Pope Sixtus II., or Xystus, as Dean Milman
calls him.   In the fierce persecution which marked the
reign of Valerian, he was seized by the Imperial Guards
and beheaded in this cemetery, with all his priests and
deacons (A.D. 258). As for that of Praetextatus, it is
the oldest with which we are acquainted, and the first
to which the ancient records give the name of Catacomb.
In a chapel here, according to an old tradition, were
deposited the bodies of St. Peter and St. Paul.

We may also mention :—

Under the *Via Aurelia:* the cemeteries of Calepodius, or S.
Calepodius, of the church of San Pancrazio, of Pope Julius, of SS.
Processus and Martinian or of S. Agatha.

Under the *Via Portuensis:* those of S. Felix, Pontianus, or Abdon
and Sennen, and of Generosa.

Under the *Via Ostiensis:* those of SS. Felix and Adauctes or of
Comodilla, of S. Timotheus, of S. Zeno.

Under the *Via Ardeatina:* that of S. Petronilla.

Under the *Via Appia:* those of Mars, Marcellinus, Damasus, and
S. Zephyrinus.

Under the *Via Latina:* those of Apronian, Gordian and Epimachus,
S. Simplicianus, Servilianus, Quartus and Quintus, Tertullian.

Under the *Viæ Labicana* and *Prænestina:* those of Tiburtius,
Marcellinus, Petrus, S. Helena, Claudius, Nicostratus, Castor, Sym-
phorian, Castulus, Zoticas.

Under the *Via Tiburtina* or of Tivoli : that of S. Cyriaca.

Under the *Via Nomentana :* the cemetery *ad Nymphas,* those of
Niomedes, Pope Alexander, Primus, Felicianus.

Under the *Via Salaria:* those of S. Priscilla, S. Felicita, Alexander, Vitalis, Martial, Chrysantes and Daria, Novella, Ostrianus,
S. Hilarius, Thrason, Saturninus, Hermes, Basilius, Protus, Hya-
cinthus.

Under the *Via Flaminia:* the cemeteries of S. Valentinus and Pope
Julius, &c.

Finally, in 1864, the entrance was discovered of one of the most ancient of the Roman cemeteries, that of *Domitilla*. This entrance has completely overthrown the popular notions of the catacombs. It is a gate of simple and classical architecture, whose style denotes a good epoch of the art. Above the pediment is visible the plan of an inscription which has long since disappeared. Through the gateway we pass into a vestibule enriched with graceful paintings, skilfully executed, of fresh and rural landscapes. It is like a corner of Pompeii, says Rossi. On either side of the vestibule extends a chamber designed for the funeral repasts or as a guard-room. All this part of the cemetery of Domitilla was raised above the ground, and was necessarily visible to every eye. It appears, according to him, to date from the reign of Vespasian or Titus.

The reader will probably ask, Who was Domitilla?

She was the niece of the Emperor Domitian, and the wife of one of his cousins-german, Flavius Clemens, the peaceful and unambitious son of Flavius Sabinus.* Both husband and wife seem to have embraced Christianity; and having excited the jealous suspicion of the emperor, were accused of atheism and Jewish manners. Clemens was put to death, and thus became the first martyr of the imperial blood. Domitilla was banished to the desert island, either of Pontia or Pandataria. But on the accession of Nerva to the throne these sentences were reversed. The exiles were recalled; and an act prohibiting all accusations of Jewish manners, seems, as Dean Milman remarks, to have been designed as a peace-offering for the execution of Clemens, and for the especial protection of the Christians.

* Suetonius, "Domitian," c. xv.

The galleries of the cemeteries have generally no other decoration than their niches, which are excavated one above another in several rows, and closed up with huge

bricks, or fragments of marble cemented together in a way that now defies imitation. These niches were all blocked up, because the cemeteries being always open to the visits of the faithful, it was needful to protect the dead from irreverent curiosity or indiscreet enthusiasm. In the Jewish catacombs, on the contrary, which were opened only when an interment took place, the guardians were contented with rolling a stone to the entrance of the vault.

The tombs of personages of rank or wealth are surmounted by an *arcosolium*, or dome-shaped head; and the *cubicula*, or chambers, enclosing these tombs are generally coated with stucco and ornamented with paintings—the most ancient being embellished with profane ornament, and others exhibiting a curious mixture of pagan traditions and Christian subjects.

Boissier remarks, that when we examine the best pictures on the walls of the catacombs, we are immediately reminded of those which decorate the walls of Pompeii. There are the same graceful borders, the same birds, the same flowers, the same rural scenes, with the same little winged genii carrying clusters of grapes or twining

A VIEW IN THE CATACOMBS OF ROME.
(After Rossi.)

wreaths of the vine. The illusion, as he says, would be complete, were it not for the frequent introduction of veiled women, praying, with clasped hands and bowed heads, their serene and devout attitude suiting so appropriately the Christian sculptures. The Christians were satisfied with reproducing such of the ancient pictures as could be applied, by a certain elasticity of interpretation, to the new doctrines. For example: they copied the fable of Orpheus, referring it to the Messianic prophecy; and that of Ulysses and the Sirens, explaining it by the necessity of resisting temptation. The very image of the Good Shepherd, of such frequent occurrence in the catacombs, and then as now the favourite figure under which the Saviour was and is represented, seems to have been adapted, says Boissier, from a heathen source; though, we may add, in pastoral ages and pastoral countries such an image would necessarily be familiar to all men, and might as readily suggest itself to the Christian as to the pagan.

A great number of articles have been discovered in the catacombs, which formerly belonged to the dead, and were buried with them. This, as we know, was a practice common to all infant communities; and we owe to it much of our knowledge of the habits and manners of our Northern ancestors. The Christian Museum at Rome contains a quantity of these interesting memorials: children's playthings, such as little ivory or bone dolls, tiny masks and bells; jewels, precious stuffs, combs of ivory or boxwood, rings, necklaces and bracelets, pouncet-boxes, vases, mirrors and other toilet articles, and a variety of household utensils, such as earthen and glass vessels, and lamps of earth, bronze, silver, and even amber.

We have now to speak of the *inscriptions* which may
still be deciphered in these gloomy galleries. Generally
they are traced on tablets of marble, or on the bricks
used for blocking up the tombs. Nearly all are confined
to the name of the dead and the date of burial, without
any mention of their social position. It is rarely even
that the tombs of the priests and bishops, or those of the
martyrs, are pointed out by any suitable epitaph to the
pious attention of the faithful.

To this sober simplicity of epigraphy, so unlike our
modern mania for emblazoning the supposed virtues of
the dead and recording their worldly honours, it is due
that antiquaries cannot fix with any degree of preciseness
the age of the different cemeteries. They are forced to
conjecture it: sometimes from the form of the letters and
the nature of the work ; sometimes from the very names
(for names change with the times) ; sometimes, and most
satisfactorily, from the style and comparative excellence
of the frescoes which cover certain chambers. Everywhere you see upon the bricks a branch of palm, with the
symbol XP painted or engraved : this is generally interpreted as *pro Christo*. It appears, however, to have been
in use before the era of our Lord. The Abbé Bencini
pretends that it is composed of the two Greek letters X
and P, under which was hidden some mystic meaning ;
but no one, it may be affirmed, can really explain them.
Whatever their early use, they were unquestionably
adopted by the early Christians as the first two letters of
the sacred name of their Master.

Occasionally, but very rarely, the inscriptions are not
content with recording the name of the dead and the date
of interment, but also contain some formulæ, some invo-

cations, which recall, in a surprising manner, the profane inscriptions. Thus, we frequently meet with the pagan invocation to the manes or spirits of the dead (*diis manibus*). And among other formulæ the following frequently recur: "Live in peace," which is of Jewish origin; and another which, at the first glance, seems still more singular, "May God give you refreshment!" Tertullian informs us that the latter formula was the prayer which the votaries of Osiris caused to be engraved upon their tombs.

The early Christians were not artists, and we need not wonder that the emblems we meet with in the catacombs are frequently of the simplest design and simplest execution. A recent English writer says: "Besides other tokens of poverty and ignorance, you find, ever and anon, upon a tombstone, the rude effigy of some animal. Here is a lion on a stone. What does it mean? Looking at the epitaph, you find that the occupant of the grave was called Leo: his relatives were too ignorant to read his name, but they could discover his grave by the lion. Here, on another, you find an ass: looking to the inscription, it proves that a person named Onager had there his resting-place; and as *onager* means 'a wild ass,' his friends, who could not read, would find his grave by the picture that answered to his name."

The symbol of a ship in full sail is sometimes found in the catacombs, just as you find it on the tombs of Pompeii; but in the latter case it merely illustrates the brevity of human life, in the former it indicates the voyage of the soul to "another and a better world." So, too, the anchor occurs as the emblem of hope and constancy; occasionally in conjunction with the dolphin, which is

said to be "the hieroglyphic of swiftness." But more
common than ship, anchor, or dolphin, than dove or
palm-branch, is the figure of a fish, generally with the
Greek word underneath it, $\iota\chi\theta\dot{\upsilon}s$. Now the fish, born in
the water, was a symbol of the Christian's new birth in
baptism ; while the word consists of letters forming the
initials of the Greek words which signify, *Jesus Christ,
Son of God, Saviour*—Ιησους Χριστος Θεου Υιος Σωτηρ.
Here was a happy token of the Christian's faith, intelli-
gible to every disciple, but absolutely without meaning to
the persecutor.

On some of the older tombs we meet with the sign of
the cross ; not, indeed, plain and simple, but with the
upper part rounded, so as to resemble the Greek *r*, P.
Others have not only this rounded cross, but also a mark
exactly like X, with P bisecting it : ☧ This is readily
explained. The Greek letter *ch* resembles our X, and is
the first letter in Χριστος (Christ). The Greek *r* resembles our P, and is the second letter in that name
before which every knee shall bow. The sign, therefore,
of the ☧ is neither more nor less than a monogram, a
portion of which we use to the present day as an abbre-
viation, writing *Xmas* for Christmas, and *Xian* for
Christian.

As years rolled on, and paganism was thrown down
from its pride of place, as peace came in the wake of protracted storm and strife, Christian art emerged from its
rude infancy, and the decoration of the tombs became of
a more graceful and elevated character. At first, it
attempted representations of wreaths, festoons, and laurel
leaves ; then of the Good Shepherd and the Lamb ; later

still, of the saints, singly or in groups; later still, of subjects from Holy Writ; and finally, of scenes in which the Godhead shines conspicuous. The favourite themes appear to have been: Adam and Eve in the Garden of Eden, Noah and the Ark, Abraham Sacrificing Isaac, Elias Ascending in the Chariot of Fire, Daniel in the Lions' Den, Jesus and the Eastern Magi, Jesus in the Temple, Jesus Restoring Sight to the Blind, the Miracle of the Loaves and Fishes, the Raising of Lazarus.

Most of the sarcophagi, and perhaps all of the urns and vases, which have been collected by hundreds and removed to the different churches of Rome, or sold and distributed

PICTURES ON THE WALLS OF THE CATACOMBS OF ST. AGNES—ROME.

over all Europe, are, as Mr. Macfarlane remarks,* in-
disputably the work of unconverted Greeks and Romans.
That such was the case, we infer from the subjects carved
or painted upon them; such as Bacchus surrounded by
Fauns, the Desertion of Ariadne, the Return of Ulysses,
the Forge of Vulcan. These sarcophagi were, at a later
date, appropriated by the Christians, who sanctified them
by adding a Christian symbol or a brief epitaph. Thus,
in the Catacomb of St. Agnes, on a sarcophagus covered
with mythological designs, are engraved these words :—

AVR. AGAPETILLA.
ANCILLA DEI.

(Aurelia Agapetilla. Handmaiden of God.) But it is
not impossible that some of the early converts, when
belonging to wealthy and patrician families, were interred
in sarcophagi blending, in this strange fashion, the
Christian inscription with the pagan sculpture. In the
early ages of the Church it did not rudely sever the ties
between the old order and the new, but adopted the old,
and sanctified it to new uses. It is thus we may account
for the fact that some of the fonts in the baptistries were
covered with poetical or legendary subjects.

If we were asked the predominant sentiment conveyed
by the epitaphs and inscriptions of the Christian catacombs, we should say it was that of REST. Evidently to
the weary and storm-beaten spirits whose dust is there
interred, as to those who mourned their departure, the
great idea presented to them by Christianity was—peace,
repose, tranquillity. They lived in a wild, fierce age of

* C. Macfarlane, "The Catacombs of Rome," pp. 126, 127.

lust, and rapine, and conquest, when the whole surface of Roman civilization was heaving with the restless convulsions of internal fires; and seeing nought but clouds around them, and hearing nothing but the hoarse alarms of war or revolution, they murmured to themselves, with that intense delight only a sad and world-sick heart *can* feel, " Come unto me, ye who are weary and heavy laden, and I will give you rest !"   After life's fitful fever, they felt that they should sleep well, until awakened by the glorious coming of their Lord and Saviour.   They longed, then, for that repose which not only contrasted so brightly with the toil and strife of their daily existence, but was doubly welcome as a prelude to eternal happiness in the immediate presence of God.

We proceed to furnish some examples :—

Satvrnina dormit in Pace.
[Saturnina sleeps in peace.]

Zoticvs hic ad dormiendvm.
[Zoticus is here to sleep.]

Galla in pace.
[Galla in peace.]

Hic in Pace Reqviescit Lavrentia. L. F. qvæ credidit Resvrrectionem.
[Here in peace lies Laurentia, daughter of Lucius, who believed in the Resurrection.]

Prima vivis in gloria Dei et in pace Domini Nostri.
[Prima, thou livest in the glory of God and in the peace of the Lord.]

Jvliæ Agapeni.
Conjvgi Dvlcissime, quae vixit annis xlv. M. iii. D. iii. Vid. et mecvm annis xxi.   Laeta in Pace.
[To Julia Agapena, my most beloved wife, who lived forty-five

years, three months, and three days, and was with me twenty-one years. Rejoicing in peace.]

Domitiana anima simplex dormit in pace.
[Domitiana, innocent soul, sleeps in peace.]

Recessit Sabbatia in somno pacis. P. An. xxvii.
[Sabbatia has departed in the sleep of peace, at the age of nearly twenty-seven.]

Benemerenti filio Calpurnio parentes fecerunt, qui vixit ann. v. M. viii. D. x. decessit in pace xiiii. Kal. Jvn.
.[To their well-deserving son Calpurnius, his parents erected this (memorial). He lived five years, eight months, and ten days, and departed in peace on the 14th of the Kalends of June.]

Scarcely less frequent than this idea of rest is that of charity towards all men, and of love and goodwill towards the Church of Christ. Others are simple memorials of friendship; others, again, express in pathetic language the mourning of those who remain for those who have gone before.

TEMPORE HADRIANI
IMPERATORIS
MARIVS ADOLESCENS DVX
MILITVM QVI SATIS VIXIT
DVM VITAM PRO XRO. CVM SAN
GVINE CONSVNSIT IN PACE
TANDEM QVIEVIT BENEMERENTES
CVM LACRIMIS ET METV POSVERVNT

[In the time of the Emperor Hadrian, the young Marius, a military commander, who lived long enough since he shed his blood for Christ, and died in peace. While he lay at rest, his friends, with tears and fears, placed this stone.]

Clavdio benemerenti stvdioso qui amabat me. Vixit an. P. M. xxv. in P.
[To Claudius, the well-deserving and studious, who loved me. He lived five-and-twenty years. In peace.]

Janvario dulci et bono filio omnibvs honorificentissimo et idoneo qvi vixit annis xxiii. M. v. D. xxii. Parentes.

[To Januarius, sweet and good son, honoured and beloved by all, who lived twenty-three years, five months, and twenty-two days. His parents.]

Jvstvs cvm scis Xpo mediante resvrget.

[Justus, who will rise with the saints, through the mediation of Christ.]

Sabbati dulcis anima pete et roga pro fratres et sodales tuos.

[Sabbatus, sweet soul, supplicate and pray for thy brothers and thy friends.]

Dormit sed vivet.

[Sleeps, but will live.]

Vitalianvs magister militvm qviescit in Domino Thesv. viii Kal. Aprilis.

[Vitalianus, a military commander, sleeps in the Lord Jesus. The 8th of the Kalends of April.]

Jvliæ Innoc. et Dulcis Mater sua sperans.

[To Julia, the innocent and sweet, her mother hoping.]

Lavrinia melle dvlcior quiesc. in pace.

[Laurinia, sweeter than honey, sleeps in peace.]

Constantia mirvm pvlchritvdinis atqve idonitatis qvæ vixit annis xviii. Men. vi. Die xvi. Constantia in Pace.

[Constantia, mirror of beauty and amiability, who lived eighteen years, six months, and sixteen days. Constantia in peace.]

Simplicio bonæ memoriæ Q. V. Ann. xxiii. D. xliii. In Pace. Fecervnt Fratres.

[Simplicius, of happy memory, who lived twenty-three years and forty-three days. In peace. His brothers erected this monument.]

Here is an inscription which forcibly reminds one of the lines on Shakespeare's tomb at Stratford-upon-Avon, —" Accurst be he who moves these stones,"—and shows how jealously the early Christians guarded against any profanation of the repose of the grave :—

MALE PEREAT INSEPVLTVS
JACEAT NON RESVRGAT
CVM JVDA PARTEM HABEAT
SI QVIS SEPVLCRVM HVNC VIOLAVERIT.

[May he perish badly, and deprived of sepulture; may he lie dead
and never rise; may he have part with Judas, who shall violate this
tomb.]

In the following epitaph (of the third century) a husband mourns for a beloved wife, but mourns, nevertheless, with the firm hopefulness of a Christian :—

" My sorrow will ever weigh upon me; may it be mine to behold
in sleep your revered countenance. O my wife Albana, the chaste
and modest, I am left alone in my grief. Our divine Maker gave
you to me as a sacred boon. You, well-deserving one, having left
your relatives, now lie in peace. But from sleep you will arise; the
rest granted to you is temporary. She lived forty-five years, five
months, and thirteen days: buried in peace. Placus, her husband,
erected this memorial."

We quote two or three inscriptions from the tombs of
martyrs :—

" Primitius, in peace, after much suffering. He lived thirty-eight
years, more or less. His wife raised this stone to her dearest husband, the well-deserving."
" Here lies Gordianus, deputy of Gaul, who was executed for the
faith, with all his family: they rest in peace. Theophila, a hand-
maid, erected this."
" Paulus was put to death in tortures, in order that he might live
in everlasting happiness."
" Launus, Christ's martyr, rests here. He suffered under Diocletian."
"Alexander is not dead, but lives above the stars, while his body
rests in this tomb. He ended his life under the Emperor Antoninus,
who, foreseeing that great benefit would flow from his services,
rendered evil for good. For while on his knees, and about to sacrifice
to the true God, he was led away to execution. O unhappy times!
in which, among holy rites and prayers, and even in caverns, we are

not safe. What can be more miserable than such a life? and what than such a death? When they cannot be buried by their friends and relatives, at length they shine in heaven. He has scarcely lived who has lived in Christian times."

Here is an inscription—one of many—referring to the purchase of the grave or burial-place :—

"Timotheus purchased this space of twelve graves, for himself and his posterity " (S. E. P. S., *sibi et posteris suis*).

From others we learn that celibacy was not practised by the early Christian priesthood :—

"The once happy daughter of the presbyter Gabinus; here is Susanna joined with her father in peace."
"Petronia, a deacon's wife, the type of modesty. In this place I laid my bones; spare your tears, beloved husband and daughters, and believe that it is forbidden to weep for one who lives in God. Buried in peace, on the third day before the nones of October, in the consulate of Festus " (A.D. 472).

In many of the martyrs' tombs have been discovered the instruments of torture from which they suffered; such as heavy chains, nails, pincers, and the like, or the stone which was fastened round the neck of the doomed Christian before he was flung into the Tiber. In a chapel of St. Peter's, at Rome, is shown a terrible instrument, called the "Iron fingers :" it is shaped like the human hand, with the fingers bent inward, as if to squeeze ; and instead of nails, these fingers are armed with long sharp points of steel, which must have inflicted the most terrible agony.

Other and pleasanter memorials of the primitive Church have also been met with ; such as the sepulchral lamps, of terra cotta or bronze, which were lighted on the occasion of an interment taking place, or during the celebra-

tion of divine worship. The body of the lamp is usually
in the form of a ship ; the handle is frequently a cross ;
and the ornaments variously consist of palm-branches,
olive-crowns, doves, or lambs.

Domestic utensils, or vessels used in the sacred rites,
as chalices or sacramental cups, and pateræ or salvers,
besides dishes, mirrors, ivory combs, or combs of boxwood, have also been found. The combs bear witness to
the ancient custom for the priest to comb out his hair
before he approached the altar. Ear-rings, necklaces,
rings, brooches, bracelets, and other articles of the femi-
nine toilet are not wanting ; nor medals, coins of gold
and silver, signet-rings, intaglios, and cameos—precious
articles thrown into the grave at the last moment by
some weeping friends, as a proof of their unceasing affec-
tion.

By the sides of many of the graves small phials have
been let into the wall, and firmly fixed with cement.
It is believed that each of these contains some drops of a
martyr's blood ; and we know, from undoubted evidence,
that the early Christians ever manifested a great anxiety
to obtain some memorial of those who died for the truth ;
rushing, often at the risk of their own lives, into the
fatal arena to dip handkerchiefs, sponges, or small pateræ
into the sacred blood. But it is not improbable that
some of these small vessels contained the milk and honey
used by the early Christians in their baptismal rites.

We cannot take leave of these famous Catacombs,
which played so important a part in the early days of
Christianity, without remarking how powerful has been
their influence even to our own times. For when it

abandoned its subterranean gloom for the light of day, Christianity still preserved a majority of the usages which it had been forced to adopt in a period of trial and persecution. Thus, the first altar was the sepulchral stone which covered the dust of the martyr put to death for his confession of the faith. Hence the custom of preserving with religious care the relics of saints under the altar-stone. The tapers and the lights which burn incessantly in Roman Catholic churches are but the memorials of the torches and lamps destined to illuminate the obscurity of the Catacombs. And the small subterranean cubicula ranged around the principal galleries served as the model and origin of the lateral chapels which, in our ancient churches,—as, for example, at Westminster Abbey,—are ranged around the nave, or fill up the aisles.

THE CATACOMBS OF NAPLES.

Next to those of Rome, the most celebrated and remarkable catacombs which we meet with in Italy are those of Naples, on the peninsula, and of Syracuse, Palermo, Girgengti, and Catania, in Sicily. We shall speak only of the more interesting.

The Neapolitan catacombs are inferior in historical importance to the Roman, but are much more beautiful and more spacious. That of Saint Januarius, for example,—I mean, the catacombs whose entrance is located in the church of that name,—are upwards of two miles in length; they extend from San Efrino Vecchio, the Capuchin church by the side of the Capo di Chino on the road to Capua, as far as the Salute, which lies on the southern side of the city.

These catacombs do not extend, like those of Rome, under the city itself, but are excavated in a neighbouring mountain, and carried through beds of an indurated pozzolana which might sometimes be mistaken for tufa.

We descend into them through four principal gates; namely, those of San Severo, Santa Maria della Sanita, the Ospicio di San Gennaro, and Santa Maria della Vita. They are arranged in three tiers or stages; but earthquakes and landslips have partly filled up the lowest tier.

We pass, at first, into a great straight gallery, eighteen feet wide, and from fourteen to fifteen feet high at the loftiest points. After awhile, the gallery begins to wind until it abuts on a kind of *carrefour*, communicating with numerous other galleries, more or less elevated, more or less narrow, which seem to have been excavated haphazard in the mountain.

In the entire breadth of the walls on either hand you perceive a prodigious quantity of cavities horizontally situated. You may see five, six, or even as many as seven set one above another. These niches are all large enough to receive a human body, though they are not all of the same size, and seem to have been adapted to the requirements of their occupants. They are suited to all ages, and some are so small that they can only have been intended for children. When the bodies had been immured in these niches, the entrance was closed with a long flat stone, or with several large tiles, set closely together, and plastered with lime and cement. The niches are now empty, and the corpses have been removed, though in a few some bones are still preserved.

At intervals, we meet in these catacombs with isolated chambers, which seem to have been appropriated as family vaults. In nearly all of these are deposited a trough-shaped coffin. Numerous tombs in these private vaults are covered with mosaics; some have not been opened.

We also remark several enclosed spaces which seem to have been used as chapels where, at the moment of inter-ment, the priest recited the prayers for the dead. The unwholesomeness of the catacombs forbids one entertain-ing the idea that they could ever have been inhabited. Two of these chapels contain altars of rough stones, and some frescoes of religious subjects executed in a very indif-ferent manner; they appear to date from the tenth century.

According to the general opinion, these vast catacombs were originally the deserted quarries from which were removed the materials employed in the construction of the beautiful Neapolis. This assertion seems to be sup-ported by their division into chambers, cul-de-sacs, carre-fours, in the midst of which have been left intact the pillars, or masses of stone requisite to support the earth above.

Employed afterwards as a pagan place of sepulture, they would appear to have been reserved, in the fourth century, for the exclusive use of the Christians. Tradi-tion asserts that those of San Gennaro have frequently served for the wholesale interment of the victims of the Plague.

THE CATACOMBS OF SYRACUSE.

The catacombs of Syracuse,—which we must not con-found, as was formerly done, with the celebrated Latomiae, —extend under the quarter of Achradina, or the "outer city." They are of earlier date than the Latomiæ, and

were consecrated at a remote period to the sepultures of
the citizens.   Having acquired a sacred character through
this particular appropriation, they served also for the
performance of initiations and mysterious ceremonies.

These remarkable catacombs are the largest and best
preserved with which we are acquainted.   They form
an immense subterranean city, regularly laid out, having
its large and small streets, its carrefours, and its open
spaces excavated in the rock.   Nothing can give a higher
idea of the greatness, power, and immense population of
ancient Syracuse, than these vast galleries, in which were
deposited the remains of that population.   A mysterious
tranquillity prevails there, which indicates the sanctuary
of repose; but these galleries, hollowed out of a hard
white rock, do not wear the sombre and majestic aspect
of those of Rome and Naples.

THE CATACOMBS OF PALERMO.

The catacombs of the Capuchin Convent of Palermo
are vast subterranean galleries situated in one of the
suburbs of that city, and divided into four regular
galleries, in whose walls a large number of vertical niches,
resembling those designed for the reception of statues,
has been wrought.   The bodies have been placed upright,
and fixed by the neck or shoulders to the wall; the
clothes which they wore previous to interment have been
left on them to rot.   The appearance of all these skeletons,
reared in their several niches, and some of them inclining
towards the gallery with strange and disordered movements, is most impressive.   We feel in these galleries,
says a contemporary traveller, mingled emotions of melan-

choly, terror, and disgust; and if the latter sentiment predominates, we are surprised to lose even the sentiment of reverence which is due to pain and death.

In certain rude coffins rest the remains of some illustrious personages, richly attired; among them a king of Tunis, who died in 1620.

On the right and left of the entrance-gate are two pictures; one of which represents the calm and gentle departure of the devout and virtuous man, and the other the terrible and agonizing death of the sinner : between the two are inscribed some stanzas commenting on the fragility of our mortal covering.

At the extremity of the great gallery is placed an altar, whose façade is a kind of mosaic composed of fragments of bones.

Finally, at the end of another gallery is a small chamber called the Oven; it is the place where the corpses were dried before they were placed in the niches.

THE CATACOMBS OF GIRGENTI.

At Agrigentum, the modern Girgenti, the walls of the city were converted into sepulchres for its heroes and patriots. You may see in the façades still extant the niches intended for this purpose; and in those which every day are being exposed to the light, we find bodies presenting an appearance of consistency, but crumbling into dust at the slightest breath. As for the principal families, they had private burial-places in subterranean corridors excavated in the flank of the neighbouring rocks, where latomiæ of great extent are still to be discovered. These rocks are of a very soft calcareous stone, full of fossil shells, which hardens on being exposed to the air.

___

THE CATACOMBS OF TUSCANY.

In Tuscany, near Volterra, are some catacombs of great extent, but in a terribly devastated condition; they are those of Bradona and Portona.

___

THE CATACOMBS OF ETRURIA.

In Etruria the antiquary meets with a perfect abundance of subterranean and sepulchral chambers, embellished with admirable work in sculpture and painting. In the mountain rising above the *Civita Tarchino*, or *Corneto*, which is presumed to be the ancient city of Tarquinii, a mile and a half to the north of Corneto, he will meet with numerous small mounds or tumuli, raised by the hand of man, and known by the local name of the Montarozzi; each one covers a separate catacomb, many of which are very large, and include a variety of streets, halls, and chambers, coated with stucco, and adorned with frescoes.

The first discoveries were made here in the last century by Mr. Byres, an Englishman resident at Rome; but no excavations were made on a systematic plan until Lucien Bonaparte purchased the principalities of Canino and Musignano, and began his valuable and interesting researches. The great explorer of Corneto, however, has been Signor Avvolta, who is of opinion that the Etrurian necropolis extended over an area of sixteen square miles, —and who conjectures, from the two thousand tombs opened in recent years, that their total number could not have been less than two million. Of the tumuli to which we have alluded, many, all which are perfect enough to be examined, appear to have had a circular base of masonry surmounted by a cone of earth. Among these tumuli Signor Avvolta discovered in 1823 the virgin tomb which first directed the attention of European archæologists to Corneto. It proved to be that of an Etruscan prince or *Lucumo*.

"I beheld," he says, "a warrior stretched on a couch of rock, and in a few minutes I saw him vanish, as it were, under my eyes ; for, as the outer air penetrated into the sepulchre, the armour, thoroughly oxydized, crumbled away into the minutest particles ; so that in a short time scarcely a vestige of what I had seen was left on the couch. So great was my astonishment, that it would be impossible for me to express the effect upon my mind produced by this sight ; but I can safely assert that it was the happiest moment of my life."

The principal painted tombs are shown to travellers in the following order :—

1. *Grotta Querciola*, discovered in 1831 : the largest and most magnificent, and finely embellished with paintings of banquets, games, boar-hunts, dances, a love-scene, and the like ; life-pictures of the old Etruscan world, not less valuable for their fidelity and spirit than the sculptures of the great rock-tombs of ancient Egypt.

2. *Grotta del Triclinio*, or *Tomba Marzi*, discovered in 1830. The brilliant frescoes here depict a funeral banquet, with several male and female figures reclining on *triclinia* or couches.

3. *Grotta del Morto*, discovered in 1832. A female, named *Thanaucil*, and a youth named *Enel*, are represented as laying out the dead body of an old man, named *Thanarsaia*, while two men, standing by, are wringing their hands in frantic grief.

4. *Grotta del Tifone*, discovered in 1832, has a roof supported by a square pillar, bearing on three of its sides the figure of the Typhon,

or Angel of Death, from which it takes its name. "The sides of the chamber," says a writer in Murray's "Rome," "have three ledges, one over the other, on which eight sarcophagi still remain, with recumbent figures on the lids. Two of them are Roman with Latin inscriptions, supposed to be those of persons descended from the ancient Etruscan family of Pompus, the *stirps* probably of the Roman family of Pompeius. The typhon represented here is a winged figure, with extended arms, supporting a cornice with his hands, the lower extremities terminating in serpents. On the right wall is one of the most remarkable paintings at Tarquinii, a procession of souls with good and evil genii, the tallest figure being nearly six feet in height, and all the others as large as life. The evil genius, or the Etruscan Charon, is black, with his head wreathed with serpents; he holds an enormous hammer in one hand, and the other, which terminates in a claw, is fastened on the shoulder of a youth. A female figure, still bearing marks of great beauty, and evidently representing the spirit of the deceased, follows, attended by another evil genius, with a serpent twined around his head. Over the head of the youth are inscribed the words *Laris Pumpus Arnthal Clan Cechase*—or Lars Pompeius, the son of Aruns."

5. *Grotta del Cardinale*, first discovered in 1699, rediscovered in 1760 by our countryman Mr. Byres, reopened in 1780 by Cardinal Garampi, and made generally known by Micali in 1808. This tomb, the largest known, consists of a single chamber, fifty-four feet on each side, with a roof supported on four square pillars, ornamented with medallions. The subject of the frieze reminds the spectator of some of the Egyptian frescoes; groups of good and evil spirits are conveying in a chariot the soul of the dead to judgment.

6. *Grotta delle Bighe*, discovered in 1827. The paintings are said to be in the purest style of Greek art. They represent dances and chariot-races; gymnastic sports, serpent charmers, and a funeral banquet; and vividly bring before us the manners and social life of the old Etruscan people.

7. *Grotta del Mare*, so named from its representation of a group of sea-horses.

8. *Grotta del Barone*, or *Grotta Kestner*, discovered by Baron Stackelberg and Chevalier Kestner in 1827. The paintings here are remarkable for their interest and brilliancy.

9. *Grotta Francesca*, or the *Grotta Giustiniani*, discovered by the Chevalier Kestner in 1833, was enriched with delineations of the sports and games celebrated at the Etruscan funerals.

10. *Grotta della Scrofa Nera* is so called from a spirited representation of the hunt of a black wild sow by two huntsmen and several dogs.

11. *Grotta delle Iscrizioni*, discovered in 1827. This is described as one of the most interesting of the series. "Over the door are two panthers, and in each angle of the pediment is a recumbent fawn with a goose at his feet. In the opposite pediment are two lions, two deer, and two panthers, all parti-coloured. On the right of the entrance is a group of two figures; one representing an old man holding a forked rod, the other a boy about to lay a fish upon a low stool, or altar, as it is considered by those who suppose the old man to be the god of chastity, and the whole scene to represent a sacrifice to him. On the left wall are two men playing at dice at a hollow table, two men boxing with the cestus, and two wrestlers. A false door in the wall separates these from a procession of four horsemen and numerous attendants on foot, with dogs, &c., who appear to have just returned from a race; the forms of the horses surpass anything ever imagined by a modern horse-breeder. A bacchic dance fills the next space, with dancers and numerous attendants bearing vases and wine-jugs; and beyond the second false door the space is occupied by a bearded figure, attended by a slave bearing boughs of trees in his hand. These paintings, by their hard outline and exaggerated details, bear evidence of their high antiquity, and are probably the oldest which are now accessible in this locality. Almost all the figures are naked or nearly so, and almost every one of them bears an inscription; but although the letters are still legible, the meaning of the words is either altogether unknown, or a matter of conjecture. Copies of the paintings are preserved in the *Museo Gregoriano* of the Vatican, and in the British Museum."

Another remarkable Etrurian necropolis exists at *Cervetri* (the ancient *Agylla*, or *Caere*), twenty-seven miles from Rome. Cervetri is the representative of a city which was founded at least thirteen centuries before the Christian era by the Pelasgi in conjunction with the aborigines; which was afterwards captured by the Etruscans; and for some generations enjoyed a high prosperity.

The attention of antiquaries was first directed to the sepulchres of its necropolis, which is excavated in the hill called *La Banditaccia*, about 1829; but the most remark-able tombs were not opened until 1836, 1845, and 1846. They are named Grotta della Sedia, Tomb of the Tar-quins, Grotta delle Sedie e Scudi, Grotta del Triclinio, Grotta dei Pilastri, La Grotta delle Urne, and Grotta Torlonia. Their characteristics do not differ from those of the tombs of Corneto, but the relics discovered in them have proved of far higher value.

THE LATOMIAE OF SYRACUSE.

The quarries of Syracuse, its *Latomiae* or *Lautumiae*, are mentioned by Cicero, in his superb oration against Verres, as among the most remarkable objects in the city. There can be no doubt, says Bunbury, that they were originally designed merely as quarries for the extraction of the soft limestone of which the whole table-land consists, and which makes an excellent building stone; but from the manner in which they were worked, being sunk to a considerable depth, without any outlet on a level, they were found places of such security, that from an early period they were employed as prisons. Thus, after the Athenian expedition, continues our authority, the whole number of Athenian captives, more than seven thousand in number, were imprisoned in these quarries; and they were used for the same purpose under successive despots and tyrants. Not only captives, but criminals, and the unfortunate victims of his hatred and vengeance, were imprisoned here by Dionysius the tyrant; and one of them preserves the name of the celebrated poet Philo-menes, who was condemned to captivity for the double crime of having criticised the monarch's verses and pleased his mistress. And the story runs, that after his release he was again summoned by the tyrant to pronounce his opinion on a fresh effort of the royal muse. Rather than do violence to his conscience, or profane his dignity as a poet, he exclaimed, "Carry me back to the quarries!"

Like the catacombs, these immense excavations are of very ancient date, but no longer inspire either fear or horror. The ravages of Time have but rendered them more picturesque. The pillars formerly carved out of the living rock to support the roof have assumed the form of immense stalactites.

The Latomiae are ten or twelve in number, and vary greatly in importance. One of the most interesting, dominated over by a Capuchin convent, of which it forms the singular garden, owes its transformation not only to Time, but to the prolonged patience of the devout and peaceful hermits who, year after year, did not cease with assiduous labour to invoke the riches and fresh vegetation of Nature from the barren rock. The waters conveyed thither by the aqueducts of old for the use of prisoners still filter through the fissures of the calcareous rock, and encourage the growth of flowers and verdure.

The most celebrated and the largest Latomia, and the most interesting next to that of the Capuchins', of which we have just spoken, now bears the various names of "Paradise," the "Latomia of the Ropemakers," and the "Ear of Dionysius." It is situated between the quarters of Tycha and Achradina, and hollowed out of the escarpment which separates Neapolis from the district along the port of Tycha. The name of "Paradise" which is sometimes given to it refers to the gardens formerly planted

in it: these were not less carefully tended than the gardens
of the Capuchins, though not equalling them in variety
and freshness. It is called the "Latomia of the Ropemakers" because some rope-works have been opened beneath its gloomy roof. And lastly, it is called, or rather

THE LATOMIAE OF SYRACUSE.

one of its recesses is called, the "Ear of Dionysius," in reference to a groundless tradition, originating in the sixteenth century, and suggested by a remarkable peculiarity
in its natural conformation.

The recess, seventy feet high at the mouth, and one

EAR OF DIONYSIUS—SYRACUSE.

hundred feet deep, is so fashioned that as it penetrates into the earth it sinks lower and lower, and describes a double curve or S. This arrangement, like that of an auricular duct, gives rise to astonishing acoustic effects : words whispered in a low voice at the bottom of the grotto are repeated very distinctly at its mouth ; a piece of paper shaken to and fro produces a sound like that of a hurricane ; and the report of a pistol reverberates like a deafening peal of thunder.   Now, toward the top of the external opening,—which terminates in a vaulted roof,—

INTERIOR OF CAVE OF DIONYSIUS—
SYRACUSE.

you will find a square aperture and a kind of little cell, as well as a small louvre, or dormer-window, communicating with the interior of the grotto.   It is pretended that Dionysius, by some secret staircase, descended from his palace into this little chamber, and, owing to the acoustic properties of the cavern, overheard the conversations and surprised the secrets of his prisoners.

Some travellers, in their curiosity to verify a fact whose historical truth is not sufficiently established by the mere configuration of the cavern, have caused themselves to be hauled up with ropes to the supposed retirement of the tyrant ; and, by so doing, have become witnesses to the curious acoustic phenomena, which they could have heard just as clearly in the depths of the grotto.

<hr />

THE CAVE OF THE CUMAEAN SIBYL.

Ennemöser tells us, in his " History of Magic," that by the word *Sibyl* we are to understand a pythoness, or

"oracular woman, who, informed by the Divine spirit,
foretold future events." Modern scepticism will be more
inclined to regard her as the agent of the impostures of
an astute and unscrupulous priesthood, who availed themselves of their superior knowledge to impose upon the
imaginations of the credulous.

The number of the Sibyls of antiquity is differently
given : Varro speaks of ten ; Aelian, of four ; Pliny and
Solinus, of three. Generally, Varro's computation is
accepted as correct ; and the ten Sibyls are then said to be
—the Babylonian, the Libyan, the Delphian, the Cim-
merian, the Erythraean, the Samian, the Cumaean, the
Trojan, the Phrygian, and the Tiburtine. Of these the
most famous is, undoubtedly, the Cumaean, whom Aris-
totle identifies with the Erythraean, and who is personally
known by the names of Herophile, Demo, Phemonoë,
Deiphobe, Demophile, and Amalthaea. To the classical
student she is familiar from the prominent part she plays
in the sixth book of the "Aeneid," where she conducts the
poet into the underground world. He describes her in
picturesque language :—*

> " But to the height Aeneas hies
>   Where Phoebus holds his seat,
> And seeks the cave of wondrous size,
>   The Sibyl's dread retreat,
> The Sibyl, whom the Delian seer
> Inspires to see the future clear,
>   And fills with frenzy's heat ;
> The grove they enter, and behold
> Above their heads a roof of gold....
>
> "The sacred threshold now they trod :
> 'Pray for our answer ! pray ! the god,'
>   She cries, 'the god is nigh !'
> And as before the doors in view
> She stands, her visage pales its hue,
>   Her locks dishevelled fly,

* The "Aeneid," translated by Professor Conington, book vi.

> Her breath comes thick, her wild heart glows,
> Dilating as the madness grows;
> Her form looks larger to the eye,
> Unearthly peals her deep-toned cry,
> As breathing nearer and more near,
> The god comes rushing on his seer."

According to Plutarch, the Cumaean Sibyl foretold the great eruption of Vesuvius in 71 A.D., when Pompeii and Herculaneum perished; and some of the early Christian writers were induced, in their enthusiasm, to interpret some of her supposed oracular utterances as referring to the advent of the Saviour. Thus, they considered the well-known lines of Virgil, in his fourth *Eclogue*, to be a Messianic prediction :— *

> "The last great age, foretold by sacred rhymes,
> Renews its finished course; Saturnian times
> Roll round again, and mighty years, begun
> From their first orb, in radiant circles run.
> The base degenerate iron offspring ends;
> A golden progeny from heaven descends;
> O chaste Lucina, speed the mother's pains:
> And haste the glorious birth; thy own Apollo reigns!
> The son shall lead the life of gods, and be
> By gods and heroes seen, and gods and heroes see.
> The jarring nations he in peace shall bind,
> And with paternal virtues rule mankind."

It is not at all impossible that some faint echo of the Jewish belief in a coming Messiah, who was to inaugurate an era of felicity, reached the priests and poets of ancient Rome; and we know, in fact, that a general restlessness extended through the civilized world for half a century before the birth of Christ. But, assuredly, in the lines we have quoted there is nothing more than that graceful conception of a purer and more peaceful age which is common to most poetical imaginations.

* Virgil, *Eclogue* iv., translated by Dryden, who adds: "Many of the verses are translated from one of the Sibyls who prophesied of our Saviour's birth."

The abodes of the Sibyls are described as, for the most part, remote and quiet places, especially caves, as was the case with the Oracles in Greece; and in Boeotia, which abounded in such caves and lairs, according to Plutarch, the chief oracles were found. Near Cumae, in Italy, the whole country was volcanic; steaming waters and sulphurous vapours frequently rendered them inaccessible to the wanderer, and at all times predisposed him for the influence of the spells and juggleries of the priesthood. It was commonly believed that the vapours of the Grotto del Cane and the Lake of Avernus were of so fatal a nature that even the birds when they approached those places were stricken dead. In what more suitable locality could an oracle be established?

The grotto or cave of the Cumaean Sibyl is still pointed out at Cumae, near Naples. It is in nowise remarkable in its dimensions or its natural decorations; the bottom is occupied by a kind of basin, resembling the crater of an ancient volcano, and which the incessant infiltrations keep half filled with water. The explorer, therefore, is compelled to mount on the shoulders of his guide to reach unencumbered the fissure or crevice through which the Sibyl formulated to the inquirer the secrets of his destiny. The prophetic orifice is surrounded by numerous natural cavities, which the hand of man has evidently modified and adapted to the use of the pseudo-prophetess and her priests. There is also shown, in the upper part of the cave, a secret entrance, reserved, it is said, for the great and wealthy when they might wish to consult the Sibyl.

The lateral apertures and subterranean passages surrounding the Sibyl's cave, and all excavated in the solid tufa which composes the hill of the Acropolis,

have been identified with the "hundred mouths" spoken
of by Virgil :—

> "Quō lati ducunt aditus centum, ostia centum,
> Unde ruunt totidem voces, responsa Sibyllae."

> The hundred mouths whence rush
> The Sibyl's answers in a hundred voices.

Justin Martyr describes in the following terms a visit
which he paid to the Sibylline retreat : "Being at Cumae,"
he says, "we saw a large basilica dug out of the rock,
where they said the Sibyl had pronounced her oracles. It
contained in the centre three large caverns, which had
served for the lustrations of the Sibyl, who afterwards retired into the innermost part of the basilica (τῆς βασιλικῆς
οἶκον), and there, from an elevated throne, uttered her
predictions of the future."

———

THE GROTTO OF NEPTUNE.

Tivoli, the ancient Tibur, situated about eighteen miles
from Rome, is endeared to the artist for its natural
beauties, to the scholar by its classical associations. Who
could fail to regard with peculiar interest the ancient city
celebrated by Virgil and Ovid, or the scenery immortalized
by the lyrics of Horace, or the shades which Catullus and
Propertius have commemorated, and where the statesmen
and philosophers of Rome loved to retreat? It was at
Tibur that the great Latin lyrist would fain have spent a
serene old age :—

> "Tibur Argeo positum colono,
> Sit meae sedes utinam senectae ;
> Sit modus lasso maris et viarum
> Militiaeque." [*]

[*] Horace, "Odes," book II vi 5.

THE RAVINE AND FALLS AT TIVOLI

[Tibur, planted by an Argive colony, may become, I hope, the seat of my old age; a limit of wandering unto me, spent with the fatigues of ocean, land, and military service.]

No other place was so fair to his partial eyes :—

"Me nec tam patiens Lacedaemon,
Nec tam Larissae percussit campus opimae,
Quam domus Albuneae resonantis,
Et praeceps Anio, et Tiburni lucus, et uda
Mobilibus pomaria rivis." *

[Me neither the enduring Lacedaemon, nor the plain of fertile Larissa, has
struck with so much admiration as the home of Albunea re-echoing (with the
roar of waters), and the headlong Anio, and the grove of Tiburnus, and the
orchards fed by rapid streams.]

But of the groves, temples, and waterfalls which excite
the admiration of the modern tourist, as they did of the
ancient poet, we have not now to speak.   Our concern is
wholly with one of its curiosities,—the so-called *Grotto of
Neptune,* which commands a romantic view of the descent
of the Anio, though the recent alterations in the course of
that river (executed by the engineer Folchi in 1834) have
deprived it of much of its interest.   It is excavated in
the travertine rock, at the bottom of the precipice over
which the waters of the Anio formerly poured in foam
and thunder; and its recesses incessantly repeat their
noisy echoes.

One of the "sights" of Tivoli is the illumination of
this grotto by means of torches and Bengal lights.

THE GROTTO AZZURRA, OR BLUE GROTTO.

If there is anything in the Gulf of Naples, says a contemporary writer, which can dispute with Vesuvius the
first impression of the traveller, it is the beautiful and
picturesque appearance of the island of Capri, the ancient
Capreae.   It is true that the memories of Tiberius and his
savage lusts are inseparably associated with the spot, and
rise before the imagination like phantoms which no spell

* Horace, "Odes," book i. vii. 13.

THE GROTTO AZZURRA—CAPRI.

can exorcise; but under the gentle influence of a nature at once radiant and magnificent they lose much of their grim power, and we are content to give ourselves up to' the enjoyment of the Present without a too anxious consideration of the Past.

The Grotto Azzurra is situated about midway between the Marina di Capri and the Punta di Vitareto, the northwest extremity of the island. It can only be approached when the sea is perfectly calm, for the rocky arch which forms the entrance does not exceed three feet in height, and is so surrounded with precipices as not easily to be detected. On entering the interior you find yourself in a fairy scene, which recalls the fancies of the early magicians or "the poetical creations of the Arabian Nights." Wall, and roof, and water shine with a glorious and intensely blue colour, a kind of unearthly and weird splendour; the effect being due to the entrance of the external light, refracted upwards into the grotto. The length is 165 feet; the maximum breadth, about 100 feet; the highest part of the vault about 40 feet above the sea-level; and the depth of water about eight fathoms.

All travellers agree in asserting that it is impossible to give an idea of the magical charm which clothes and embellishes this recess. Figure to yourself, says Alexander Dumas, an immense cavern wholly of azure, as if Providence had been pleased to construct a pavilion out of some remnant of the firmament; a water so limpid, so transparent, so pure, that it seems to float upon the denser air; clusters of stalactites, like reversed pyramids, hanging from the roof; at bottom, a golden sand mingled with submarine vegetation; and along the sides, where the

waters incessantly roll and plash, stems of coral throwing
out their fantastic and resplendent branches.

The celebrated composer, Felix Mendelssohn, has also
given in his "Letters" a description as accurate as it is
interesting of this wonder of the sea.

"The sunlight," he says, "broken and deadened by the
water, produces the most marvellous effects. The huge
rocks are entirely lit up by a kind of crepuscular azure
and emerald sheen, which has almost the character of
moonlight; nevertheless, you can easily distinguish the
slightest chinks and angles. As for the sea, it is everywhere penetrated by the rays of the sun, so that the black
bark glides over a clear and brilliant surface. The water
is of the most dazzling blue that I have ever seen, without any shadow or obscurity. You might call it a disc
of the clearest crystal; and, as the sun softly traverses
the liquid mass, you can distinctly discern whatever
passes underneath the water, and the sea reveals itself
with all its denizens. You see the corals and polypes
attached to the rocks; and, at great depths, fishes of all
kinds dart to and fro, and cross in all directions. The
rocks appear gloomier and yet gloomier as they shoot
downwards, and at the point where the water reaches
them they assume a deep black hue; but you see beneath
them the shining waters with their living freight. Each
stroke of the oar awakens the most astonishing echoes;
and as you pass along the sides you are constantly dis-
covering quite a new creation. I wish that you could see
this, writes the great musician, for assuredly it is something magical. If you turn yourself in the direction of
the entrance, the daylight which traverses it seems of a
yellowish red, but it only penetrates two or three yards

into the interior; so that you are there on the sea all alone, with a rocky vault above, with your own sun to yourself; it seems to you that you might, so to speak, accustom yourself to live under water." *

This beautiful scene is nowhere mentioned in the writers of antiquity. The common story runs, that it was discovered by two Englishmen in 1822, while bathing; but the truth is, that it is described by Capaccio as far back as 1605, and by Addison, who visited Italy in 1701, and that it was re-discovered by a fisherman of the island, named Ferrara, who was rewarded by the Neapolitan government with a small pension.

On the south side of the island lies the Green Grotto (*Grotta Verde*), where, as the name suggests, the rocks assume a beautiful emerald colour. Its dimensions, however, are inconsiderable, and it cannot for one moment compete in interest or splendour with the Grotto Azzurra.

THE GROTTO OF POSILIPO.

The *Posilipo* (in Italian, *Monte di Posilippo*) is a mountain of ancient Campania, which fronts on one side towards the sea of Pozzuoli, and on the other towards the city of Naples. It forms a creek or cove in the famous Parthenopean Bay by stretching out into the sea as if to join the little island of Nisida, which seems to have been detached from it by the incessant action of the waters. From one end to the other this mountain is pierced by a grotto or tunnel, about 3000 feet in length, from 30 feet to 80 in height, and 28 feet in breadth. The road from Naples to Pozzuoli is carried through it; and it forms

* "Lettres inédites de Mendelsohn" (translated by Rolland), L xxxl., p. 154.

an agreeable and romantic covered promenade, to which
the only objection is that the view is necessarily limited,
and that the wayfarer is often choked with dust; while,
as the road is not very wide, he has to press closely up to
one side, to escape collisions with vehicles coming in the
opposite direction. Should any little accident occur, it
is not easily remedied in the prevailing obscurity; and,
therefore, to avoid as far as possible any dangerous
encounters, he should generally keep to the right,—that
is, on the side of the mountain,—when coming *from*
Naples; and to the left,—that is, on the side of the sea,
—when going *towards* it.

Twice a year, in the months of February and October,
the last rays of the sun sweep through the whole grotto
for a few minutes. The effect is then very fine and impressive, and seems to proceed from some magical incan-
tation. At all other times a gloomy twilight reigns by
day, but at night a sufficient illumination is produced by
the lamps which hang at intervals from the rude rough
roof of the tunnel.

It is a singular spectacle, says a writer, to see in a
feebly transparent obscurity the agitation which incessantly prevails in this long gallery. You cannot hear, at
first, without a feeling of alarm, the rattle of vehicles of
all kinds coming from the opposite direction, the clash of
horses' hoofs and their frequent neighing, the tramp and
bellow of cattle, the bleating of sheep, the shouts of drivers
and peasants,—all these confused noises rebounding upon
the roof, and echoing again and again in the deep depres-
sions and fissures which occur at intervals on either side.

It is impossible to ascertain the date or the architect

GROTTO OF POSILIPI.

of this curious work.   The Greek geographer Strabo, who
died in the reign of Tiberius (about 25 A.D.), and Seneca,
the Roman philosopher (65 A.D.), both refer to it in their

writings. Originally it seems to have been a quarry
which was afterwards converted into a practicable tunnel
The mouth of it, choked up with thorns and brambles
was cleared and enlarged by Alphonso I., King of Naple:
and Aragon, by whose order the air-shafts also were con
structed. Some considerable repairs were undertaken by
Pedro di Toledo, Viceroy of Naples, under the Empero:
Charles V.

On reaching the extremity of the grotto, the road for a
hundred yards is bordered by high walls of rock.

Above the grotto is found a Roman tomb, or, more
correctly speaking, a *columbarium*, in which, according to
tradition, repose the ashes of the poet Virgil. It consists
of a chamber about fifteen feet square, with a vaulted
roof, and lighted by three windows. In the walls are
ten niches, like the partitions of a dove-cot (hence the
name, *columbarium*), intended for the reception of cinerary
urns ; and in the ruined wall opposite the entrance a
larger niche is just discernible.

The authenticity of this interesting monument has
been disputed by some authorities ; but the precise in
dications furnished by the classical writers, and the unin
terrupted chain of confirmatory evidence, extending from
the death of the poet of the " Aeneid " to our own days
ought to satisfy the most incredulous. Many historica
facts, whose certainty is admitted, are far from being
supported by such abundant proofs. Formerly, a laure
planted by Petrarch flourished upon the tomb ; but i
disappeared under the destructive knives of visitors of al
nations. Another, planted by Casimir Delavigne, ha:
shared the same fate But the people, in passing, make
the sign of the cross, and kneel in momentary prayer, a:

if before the relics of some famous saint; and no visitor to Naples omits to perform a pilgrimage to a shrine ever dear to the lover of true poetry.

GROTTOES OR CRYPTS OF ST. PETER OF MAESTRICHT.

It is in this section, we think, and among the remarkable subterranean works bequeathed to us by ancient Rome, that we ought to include the celebrated quarries excavated in the Petersberg, or St. Peter's Mount, a quarter of a league from Maestricht, whose principal galleries, the most interesting and the most ancient, were hewn by the Roman soldiery who occupied the formidable entrenchments on the summit of the mountain.* It is true that many generations have contributed their share in the construction of the immense labyrinth which now embraces, we are assured, an area six leagues in length by two in width; but, after all, it was the Romans who first plied the pickaxe in the sides of the rocky eminence, and it is but just to give them the honour.

You can penetrate into the crypts of Maestricht through numerous entrances, some of which, owing to the peculiar position of the citadel of Maestricht, are situated in Belgium, others in Holland.

The entrances to the crypts, on the side of the Meuse, are placed half-way down the declivity, in an apparently inaccessible locality; but, in truth, they are easily gained; and the owner of the château of Caster (*castrum*, a camp), on the summit, has caused them to be carefully

---

* Maestricht, whose name is a Dutch rendering of the Latin words, *Mosae trajectum* (or "passage of the Meuse"), was long an important Roman city, and the principal traject across the Meuse from Belgium into Germany.

cleared, and planted them with trees; so that they now form a very pleasant promenade.

Near Fort St. Peter is a second entrance, regularly designed, and built with masonry. It is visible from the Tongrès road, and has an extremely imposing aspect.

Another, but much less striking entrance, occurs in the side of the village of Cannes. It is nothing more than an opening of limited dimensions in a yellowish friable sandstone. In front of it the smiling valley of the Jaer, a tiny affluent of the Meuse; further off, the well-cultivated plains and charming village of Cannes, with its clean and well-built cottages,—form a peaceful and most delightful landscape. This entrance does not admit you into the quarries properly so called, but rather into a part which is the unaided work of nature—into a vast natural grotto, whose roof is very lofty, and which encloses immense halls and galleries in the solid rock, without a chink or cranny in their solid sides. The silence there is so profound that you can scarcely hear your own words, nor does the footfall of the visitor strike his ear,—a phenomenon due to the extreme porousness of the rock, which so completely absorbs the sound, that over an extent of six thousand five hundred yards only one echo occurs, and that is extremely feeble.

When we arrive in the quarries, properly so called, we see before us a succession of long horizontal galleries, supported by an immense number of square pillars, whose height is generally from ten to twenty feet. The number of these vast subterranean alleys, which cross each other and are prolonged in every direction, cannot be estimated at less than two thousand; the direct line from the built-up entrance, near Fort St. Peter, to the exit on the side of the Meuse, measures one league and a half.

The galleries wrought by the Roman soldiery are the most ancient. Their roof is flat, and rests upon masses of rock, about sixteen feet high, and more than twenty paces in length. They are traced on a regular plan, and cut one another at right angles; but their most noticeable feature is the extreme regularity and perfect level of the roof, which is enriched with a kind of cornice,—a cornice of the severest possible outline, but with a noble simplicity which gives to the galleries a certain monumental aspect. The tunnels excavated at a later date are ruder in every respect; the walls are roughly hewn, without regularity, and with no cornice to the roof.

Complete solitude and perfect silence reign in these gloomy vaults. Their temperature keeps at 50° F., and the air is always remarkably pure.

One of the curiosities of these quarries is the great number of cylindrical cavities you meet with. They may be compared to natural shafts or wells, either vertical or slightly oblique, from one to several feet in diameter, and filled with clay, sand, and refuse. These cavities, to which the name has been given of " Geological organs," are frequently met with in the calcareous formations, but are seldom so regular in disposition as those of Maestricht.

One of the points of intersection presents another very remarkable curiosity,—a small basin filled with water, called the *Springbronnen* (" source of living water "), which is incessantly renewed, thanks to the drops falling from the upper portion of a fossil tree fixed in the roof,

and separated from the lower part by the tools of the
quarrymen, when they were at work on the stone of
this particular locality.

Stories are told of several individuals who, having
imprudently ventured into the inextricable labyrinth
formed by the intercrossing of all these subterranean
alleys, lost their way, and died there of hunger. Among
others, four Franciscan monks are mentioned, who
perished, in 1640, in an attempt to found a hermitage in
a distant gallery. They had taken the precaution to
furnish themselves with a skein of silk, of which they
had attached one end to the entrance; but the thread
broke. In spite of the most active researches, their
bodies were not found until a week had gone by. Now-
a-days such accidents are impossible, though several
entrances to the caverns are never closed. Considerable
works were commenced while Belgium belonged to
France, and afterwards completed by the Dutch, with
the view of enlarging the principal galleries and shutting
up the lateral ones, so that without a guide, and in the
completest obscurity, a wanderer might be sure of reaching one or other of the various exits by following up the
wider galleries without diverging either right or left.
The difference in width is sufficient to guard against any
mistake.

The crypts of Maestricht have frequently furnished an
asylum to the inhabitants of the town and the surrounding country during the terrible wars which have so often
devastated the Low Countries. In 1815, the celebrated
French naturalist, Bory de St. Vincent, whose name was
inscribed on the lists of the proscribed, and who was

hunted by the police of Europe, sought a retreat in these quarries. He took the opportunity of investigating them; and published the result, in 1823, under the title of "Voyage Souterrain."

We have said that the working of these rich quarries dates from a very remote antiquity. This is proved by the inscriptions engraved upon the side walls, which are still in a state of admirable preservation. Those belonging to the Roman epoch can no longer be deciphered, because the most ancient are written nearest to the summit of the roof; but the large Roman capital letters may often be made out. Underneath these inscriptions you can trace some ill-formed characters, traditionally attributed to the Huns; which is ridiculous, since the Huns did not build, and, therefore, had no need of quarries—and, moreover, were ignorant of the art of writing. Still lower down are several rows of Gothic characters. And, in truth, the quarries were most actively worked in the Middle Ages, when the materials were required for the construction of the vast and beautiful churches which are the glory of Maestricht. Some of these superb edifices belong to the epoch when Christianity was preached in Belgium by St. Servais; and, though built of sandstone, they have braved the influences of Time and the atmosphere without losing either their colour or their consistency. A man, armed with a pocket-knife, could demolish in a day the pillars which support the tower of St. Peter of Maestricht; and yet it has been standing now for upwards of twelve centuries, and seems likely to endure for yet another twelve.

Below the Gothic inscriptions are Spanish characters,

modern when compared with the others, since they date
only from the sixteenth century, when Belgium was a
Spanish possession.   And, lastly, we come to the German
names, some of which, perhaps, have been traced by con-
temporaries; for the working of these quarries has not
been abandoned.   A considerable part of the Low
Countries still draws its building stone from their inex-
haustible recesses.   Cars, loaded with stones, issue from
the quarries by a broad and convenient road laid down
in front of the Meuse.   They easily descend to the river-
bank, where they are promptly unloaded.

The bed in which the quarries are excavated is one of
limestone, belonging to the upper cretacean series.   It
forms a powerful stratum, and rests on the white chalk;
it is a soft and yellowish limestone, about fifty feet in
thickness.   The building stone is dug out of the portions
which are most coherent; in the others, its friability
makes it much sought after for repairing roads.   Towards
the bottom it is very white, and interspersed with nod-
ules of chalcedony.

A great number of fossils have been found in the sandy
limestone of Maestricht; and especially, in 1770, the
gigantic skull of a marine reptile, now known as the
Mosasaurus.   This saurian, it is supposed, was twenty-
six feet long; and its skull, armed with a formidable
apparatus of teeth, not less than four and a half feet.   The
Natural History Museum of Maestricht contains a valuable collection of fossils found in these quarries in 1800.
It presents, too, a series of one hundred and forty
vertebræ, eighty-two of which fit into one another like a
tenon into a mortice, and some of which seem to belong

to cetaceæ, while others are more appropriate to lizards. Though they were united horizontally when discovered,

SKULL OF THE MOSASAURUS.

it is difficult to believe that they belonged to one and the same individual, for amongst them were found two teeth, one a crocodile's and the other a shark's.

GROTTOES AND CAVERNS MADE USE OF AS PLACES OF REFUGE IN THE ROMAN ERA.

History has preserved the record of a certain number of caves in various parts of Europe, where the populations living in their vicinity found a refuge from the swords of the Romans, those most implacable of conquerors.

It is thus that the Hebrew tribes would flee, with their wives and children, to the deep caverns yawning among the mountainous precipices of Palestine. But even there they were not safe from Herod's soldiers, —who were lowered into their retreats, impregnable as they seemed, in large, solid caissons suspended to chains of iron.

In reference to this subject, we may be permitted to quote a striking passage from a well-known authority :—*

"How great a part," says Dean Stanley, "the caverns of Greece played in the history and mythology of that country, is well known. In one respect, indeed, those of

DISLODGEMENT OF FUGITIVES BY HEROD'S SOLDIERS.

Palestine were never likely to have been of the same importance, because, not being stalactite, they could not so forcibly suggest to the Canaanite wanderers the images of sylvan deities, which the Grecian shepherds naturally found in the grottoes of Parnassus and Hymettus. But from other points of view we never lose sight of them. In these innumerable rents, and cavities, and holes, we see

* Dean Stanley, "Syria and Palestine," 151.

the origin of the sepulchres which still, partly natural and partly artificial, perforate the rocky walls of the Judean valleys; the long line of tombs beginning with the cave of Machpelah, and ending with the grave of Lazarus— which was 'a cave, and a stone lay upon it'—and 'the sepulchre hewn in the rock, wherein never man before was laid.' We see in them the shelter of the people of the land, in the terrible visitations of old, as when 'Lot went up out of Zoar, and dwelt in a cave;' or as when 'in the days of Uzziah, King of Judah, they fled before the earth- quake to the ravine of the mountains;' to the rocky fissures, safer, even though themselves rent by like con- vulsions, than the habitations of man. We see in them, also, the hiding-places which served sometimes for the defence of robbers and insurgents, sometimes for the re- fuge of those 'of whom the world was not worthy;' the prototype of the catacombs of the early Christians, of the caverns of the Vaudois and the Covenanters. The caves of the five kings at Makkedah; the 'caves and dens and strongholds' and 'rocks' and 'pits' and 'holes' in which the Israelites took shelter from the Midianites in the time of Gideon, from the Philistines in the time of Saul; the cleft of the cliff Etam, into which Samson went down to escape the vengeance of his enemies; the caves of David at Adullam and at Maon, and of Saul at Engedi; the cave in which Obadiah hid the prophets of the Lord; the caves of the robber-hordes above the plain of Gennesareth; the sepulchral caves of the Gadarene demoniacs; the cave of Jotapata, where Josephus and his countrymen concealed themselves in their last struggle,—continue from first to last what has truly been called the 'cave-life' of the Israelite nation."

In France, too, it would be easy to point out numerous caverns whither the Gauls fled from the pursuit of the Roman legions.

Florus, who lived at the commencement of the second century, relates that Caesar ordered his lieutenant Crassus to shut up the cunning people of Aquitaine in the caves to which they had retired (" Aquitani, callidum genus, in speluncas se recipiebant, Caesar jussit includi "). It would appear that great numbers of these unfortunate Aquitani perished in their caves, as formerly perished the Arabs of the tribe of Ouled-Riah in their grottoes of the Dahra.

Certain other peoples of Gaul, who, according to the testimony of Caesar himself, were employed in working beds of clay, iron-ore, and various mineral products, were also accustomed to seek in caves a shelter from bad weather and a refuge in time of war. And here, too, they would seem to have established their magazines of provisions, and to have stalled their cattle.

To cite but one example, we may mention that in the department of Seine-et-Oise, near Maintenon, is a grotto, or rather a subterranean gallery, the entrance of which lies on a farm of the village of Senantes. It formerly served as a retreat for the inhabitants of the district, but could not protect them from the merciless swords of the Roman soldiery. Not far from this grotto, which has been known from time immemorial, may be traced, says Nourtier, the site of a Roman camp.

This custom of dwelling in caves, or fleeing to them for sanctuary, appears to have been continued in several French provinces long after the fall of the Roman empire. We learn from Eginhard that it was in vogue in the eighth century, and that the subjects of Guaïfre, last duke of Aquitaine, sought in the caverns and ravines an occasional asylum, during their protracted struggle against King Pepin.

Though the subject is an interesting one, our limited space precludes us from entering further upon its consideration ; or we might show how the caves of Germany and Switzerland were also the refuge of the oppressed when the Roman legionaries extended the supremacy of Rome from the Apennines to the Black Forest, and from the Tiber to the Elbe.

V

𝔐𝔬𝔡𝔢𝔯𝔫 𝔗𝔦𝔪𝔢𝔰.

S in ancient times, so in modern, the chronicle furnish us with a long list of caverns at grottoes remarkable for the part they ha played in history or religion, whether they may have be consecrated by the residence or the death of some sai or some illustrious personage; whether some importa historical fact has for ever dragged them out of obliviot or, finally, whether they owe their origin to some gigant human labour. We shall follow, in describing them, th classification which seems the natural one.

GROTTO IN THE DESERT OF TEMPTATION.

This is the name given to a cavern in Palestine in whit it is supposed, though without any foundation, that ot Lord was tempted by Satan. The evangelists, in recor ing the details of the Temptation, do not even allude to cavern; but the Père Nau pretends (in his "Voyage ‹ la Terre Sainte," bk. iv., c. 4) that it is to be found on mountain of the Holy Land, whose summit is extreme elevated, and whose bottom is an abyss. He adds th this mountain, in curving from the east towards the nort presents a façade of scarped rocks which open at intervals to form several grottoes of widely different dimensions. Everybody, therefore, is at liberty to name whichever of these he pleases the Cavern of Our Saviour's Temptation.

GROTTO OF SAINT ROSALIA.

The Grotto of Saint Rosalia, the patroness of Palermo, occurs in a mountain of moderate elevation which rises on one of the sides of the roadstead of Palermo.

This mountain, now known as Monte Pellegrino, formerly bore the name of Mount Erecta, and was occupied, it is said, by the impregnable camp where Hamilcar, for five years, defied the courage and strategy of the Romans. Monte Pellegrino, after having been long neglected and deserted, suddenly became, in 1624, as the result of the semi-legendary incidents we are about to relate, the object of Sicilian veneration, and the goal of the devoutest pilgrimages.

At the expense of the state was constructed a somewhat steep but magnificent road, the *Scala*, which rises, like a staircase, from terrace to terrace, across escarpments and precipices, up to the very threshold of the sacred grotto, situated nearly at the summit of the mountain in an admirable position. And around the entrance was raised an enclosure of buildings forming a kind of court, in which were lodged the monks vowed to the *cultus* of the Palermitan saint. Finally, opposite the grotto, at the other extremity of this court, of which the escarpment of the rock forms the foundation, was erected a chapel, which was soon enriched by the costly offerings of the pilgrims.

From a small terrace near the chapel, where has stood

for many years a small hostelry devoted to the entertainment of pilgrims and travellers, you may enjoy one of the finest prospects imaginable. Nearly at the foot of the mountain you see the graceful city of Palermo and its suburbs, the *Bagaria* and the *Colle*, with their rich villas and leafy shades. Afar off winds the serpentine range of the loftiest peaks of Etna, separated from you by the whole length of the island, with its plains and streams and valleys, its vineyards and its gardens. Finally, in the direction of the sea, lie the beautiful islands of Lipari, each in its belt of deepest azure, and Stromboli, with its column of smoke darkening against the horizon.

We have now to explain the reason of the influx of pilgrims to the summit-cavern of Monte Pellegrino.

According to an ecclesiastical legend, Saint Rosalia sprang from the family of Roger, the grandson of the celebrated Tancred de Hauteville, and first king of Sicily, who lived in the early years of the twelfth century. Another legend pretends that she was the niece of King William the Good, who reigned over Sicily in the year 1150 to 1154, and to whom succeeded his son, William the Bad. Finally, other chronicles relate that she was simply the daughter of a Sicilian count, named Sinibald.

However this may be, at the age of sixteen years Saint Rosalia was endowed with the finest charms of female loveliness; and these, not less than her virtues and piety, had won her the admiration of all Sicily, when she suddenly disappeared in 1159. As no traces of her could ever afterwards be discovered, the popular super-

stition came to the conclusion that she had been raised
to heaven as

> "Something much too fair and good
> For human nature's daily food."

The legend explains her evanishment, by relating that she
had conceived an insurmountable disgust for the frivolous
life and empty gaiety of courts, and had voluntarily retired
to the obscure cavern of Monte Pellegrino, where she
spent many years in solitude and prayer.

When death at last surprised her in her self-chosen
retreat, the angels were charged with the task of burying
her, and of depositing on her sacred remains imperishable
wreaths of roses.

However, the beauty, virtues, and misfortunes of the
saint were completely effaced from the memory of the
Sicilians, until, five centuries later, Palermo fell a prey
to the horrible ravages of the plague. Its inhabitants
vainly implored the mercy of Heaven at the foot of the
holy altars. Now it happened, one day, that a citizen
renowned for his piety descended from Monte Pelegrino,
announcing that a celestial revelation had taught him
that the bones of the holy Rosalia reposed unhonoured
in a grotto of this mountain, adding that if these sacred
relics were carried thrice round the city, the contagion
would immediately cease. A deputation was despatched
to the cave ; the bones of the saint were discovered ; and,
on the following day, were transported three times round
the walls in solemn pomp. The plague was immediately
stayed.

It was in recognition of this miraculous blessing that
the inhabitants of Palermo chose Rosalia for the patron

of their city. The sacred bones were enshrined in a magnificent silver reliquary, ornamented with gems and costly work, which was solemnly deposited in the ancient cathedral of the city.

From that day, Saint Rosalia in Palermo held the place which St. Januarius occupies in Naples. Her fête, which occurs in the month of July, lasts for five days, and excites an almost incredible enthusiasm. The shrine of the patron is paraded in the principal street of the city amidst an immense concourse of people, on a car whose lofty top is on a level with the highest mansions, and which is drawn by forty mules, and filled with musicians. This superb ceremony is accompanied by horse-races— the horses either ridden by jockeys or running free, a pastime especially dear to the Palermitans—and by fairy-like illuminations.

Near the extremity of the cavern stands a statue of Saint Rosalia, who is represented as a beautiful young girl of devout inclination, adoring a cross towards which she raises her half-closed eyes. This statue comes upon you so unexpectedly and so mysteriously in its dim retreat, that, even at a few paces, you might well believe it was some young Sicilian maid lost in a religious ecstasy. A number of tiny silver lamps, suspended at intervals, shed a feeble light which enhances the illusion, and with shifting, wavering rays seem to communicate their movement to the sacred effigy. The delicate expression of the features, which breathe simplicity and resignation, the sweet tranquillity of the attitude, the pure and floating lines of the robes, captivate and charm your eye long after you have detected the secret. The head and hands have been sculptured in fine Parian marble; the robes are of gilded bronze, in which many costly gems have been incrusted.

The authors of the libretto of Meyerbeer's grand opera, *Roberto il Diavolo*, have converted the grotto of Saint Rosalia into a spacious monastery founded by the saint. And it is here that Robert, guided by Bertram, goes in quest of—

> " Le rameau toujours vert, talisman redouté,
> Qui donne la richesse et l'immortalité."

> The charmèd talisman,—th' unfading branch
> Of brightest green, which gives to its possessor
> The boon of wealth and immortality.

The statue in the grotto was the work of Gregorio Tedeschi. Another effigy stands in a strikingly picturesque situation on the brink of a tremendous precipice; a landmark for the devout mariner, who, when he comes in sight of it, crosses himself and invokes the protection of his patroness.* It was injured by lightning in 1841, but has recently been restored by Rosolino la Barbera.

NUMEROUS GROTTOES DESIGNATED UNDER DENOMINATIONS BORROWED FROM RELIGIOUS TRADITIONS.

We shall find—in France principally, but also in other European countries—a considerable number of caverns which by their names recall and preserve the superstitious fancies of the ancient world.

Nothing is more common, for example, than to meet with the "Fairies' cave," the "Dragon's cave," or the " Devil's grotto;" or to find them placed under the invo-

* Bartlett, " Pictures from Sicily," p. 250.

cation of some holy hermit, who made them his abode at some more or less distant epoch, and expelled from their dark recesses the pretended dragons or demons,—that is, the pagan superstitions, the popular tradition of which is thus preserved.

In France, a very common designation is that of *Balme*, or *Baume ;* a word which appears to belong to antiquity, and probably to the Celtic language.   We may mention the caverns of " La Grande Balme," " Notre Dame de la Balme," "La Sainte Balme," "La Sainte Baume," "Baume-les-Dames," and " Baume-les-Messieurs."   This peculiar denomination is principally found in the south and east provinces of France ; in Languedoc, Provence, Dauphiné, Franche-Comté, Bourgogne ; then in Limousin, Poitou, the Nivernais, and even in Anjou : it is also very common in Switzerland.   The use made of this word *Balma* in the " Lives of the Saints," which were written before the eleventh century, as well as by the chronicler Joinville, bears witness to its ancient origin.

We shall not here attempt a description of these interesting caverns, because, most of them being remarkable, either for their stalactitic character or for the streams which traverse and have created them, they are fully described in a companion volume specially devoted to natural phenomena of that order.*

GROTTOES USED AS SUBTERRANEAN HABITATIONS, OR AS PLACES OF REFUGE IN TIME OF WAR.

In our modern history it is easy to adduce numerous examples of caverns which have served as places of habi-

* See " Famous Caverns and Grottoes."

tation. Without referring to the natural or artificial
subterranean excavations which furnished the early hermits with retreats appropriate to their ascetic and medi-
tative life, the ancient custom of living "underground,"
peculiar at first to savage man, as Pliny reminds us—
Specus erant pro domibus—is preserved even in our own
days, and among the most civilized peoples. In many
parts of France, entire villages, including the church—
as at Rémonat, in Franche-Comté—are excavated in the

CHURCH OF RÉMONAT.

soil. Some of these grottoes served as a refuge for the
neighbouring population during the civil wars of the
Middle Ages, and more especially during those of the
Reformation.

An Italian journal very recently related that at Naples
itself, at the foot of the hill of San Martino, several hundreds of individuals lived in dark and dreary caverns.
Some of these are excavated under the declivities of
Brancaccio. You descend into them through a narrow

opening, which also permits the entrance of a sufficient amount of light to illuminate a few yards; the remainder of the cave is always in complete darkness. Yet hundreds of people live here, employed in the manufacture of cordage; they all live underground, pell-mell, without any separation of families. Some lie on a little mattress; others on a bundle of straw, with a thin and scanty coverlet. The newspaper from which we borrow these details informs us that efforts are being made to ameliorate the condition of these poor operatives.

There is not a province in France where we shall not find some examples of similar caverns, and frequently the newspapers announce the unexpected discovery of new ones. Within the last year or two an interesting communication appeared in the *Echo de la Creuse*, which will furnish the reader with a vivid idea of cave-life as it formerly existed :—

"Some days ago, in a field belonging to the commune of Saint-Sulpice-le-Donseil, a labourer found that one of his cattle had sunk into a hole. He conceived the notion of clearing out this hole; and to his great surprise discovered that it was neither more nor less than the entrance to a genuine subterranean grotto. The alarm was quickly given, and everybody hastened to visit this cavern, whose existence had been completely unknown. Its plan has been sketched by the official authorities of La Creuse, and exhibits some curious arrangements, unusual in the numerous monuments of this kind bequeathed to us by past ages. The grotto, which has been hewn out of a comparatively soft gray granite, is in an excellent state of preservation; the proof of which is its peculiar form, and the marks of tools still clearly visible in many places.

"After passing through the narrow entrance, you make your way with some difficulty down a sloping gallery, some fifteen yards in length, to a depth beneath the surface of nearly twenty feet; this portion is in the worst condition. Then you find yourself in a circular gallery, measuring about sixty-five feet in circumference, with the roof supported by a huge pillar, eighteen feet in diameter. It is worth noticing that the walls, which are hewn out of the granite, are not vertical, but convex like an egg. At nineteen feet to the left of the inclined corridor, and at an elevation of thirty inches above the level of the soil of the circular gallery, we come upon a small opening, through which it is just possible for a man to squeeze himself: it gives access to a gallery, thirty-three feet long, at the bottom of which a loftier and more spacious gallery has been begun, but, apparently, not completed. The different caves or galleries were formerly provided with three air-shafts, eight inches in diameter; but these have been partly filled up by successive landslips."

We could easily multiply our examples of caverns of this nature, for they abound in France, but shall content ourselves with enumerating the following as being, probably, the most interesting :—

At the crater of *Mont-Brul*, near St. Jean-le-Noir, or Le Centenier, in the volcanic chain of the Couërons Mountains ;

At *La Chaud de Perrier*, to the west of Issoire, on the banks of the Creuse, excavated in a volcanic earthy tufa,—in these caverns human habitations have been constructed, several of them numbering as many as seven stories ;

At the *Chaud de Corant*, on the road from Vic to Clermont, above the Martres de Vaires, excavated in a volcanic mountain, whose

summit is crowned by a magnificent colonnade of basalt upwards of
sixty-five feet in height;

At *Cournador* and at *Laval*, where they are now inhabited only
by clouds of aquatic birds, such as gulls, cormorants, and puffins;

At the village of *Cangoireau*, a short distance from Bordeaux,
where some of the caves are still inhabited by the peasants;

At *St. Chamas*, excavated in a hill of limestone, situated on the
shore of the lake of Berre: the hill has been tunnelled so as to facili-
tate communication between the two parts of the town; and the hill,
in which the industry of man has wrought out not only a series of
dwelling-places, but store-rooms for the reception of corn and oil-
mills, resembles a hive occupied by industrious bees;

At *Mont-Richard*, in the department of Loir-et-Cher, where they
exhibit the appearance of a subterranean town, and their origin dates
back, it is said, to the remotest antiquity;

At the sources of the *Ourcq*, in the department of the Aisne: the
caves, according to tradition, were the dwelling-places of the aboriginal inhabitants of the country;

At *Rolleboise*, on the left bank of the Seine: they are excavated in
a mountain of hard chalk which is relieved by numerous belts or
parallel zones of flint;

At *La Cave à Margot*, at Sauges, near Saint-Pierre-d'Erve, in the
department of the Sarthe;

At *Savonnières*, on the highroad from Tours to Chinon;

At *Rencogne* and at *Baudisi*, near La Rochefoucauld;

At *Miremont* or at *Granville*, between the towns of Sarlat and
Périgueux;

The celebrated *Grottes Demoiselles* ("Las Doumaisellas") in the
Taurach rock, above the village of Ganges, and near Saint-
Beauzile.

And those of *Loizin* and *Vubos*, in the Jura, celebrated from time
immemorial as having furnished a succession of hermits with a lonely
asylum.

A special reference seems necessary to the *caves in the
Dordogne*, because they have thrown a vivid light on the
much disputed question of the antiquity of man. They
are particularly interesting, because they seem to belong
to what has been called the "reindeer period," and tend,
therefore, to connect the later or Polished Stone Age with

the period of the river-drifts and the great extinct mammalia, such as the mammoth and mastodon. Those which have been most carefully examined are ten in number: Laugerie, La Madelaine, Les Eyzies, La Gorge d'Enfer, Le Moustier, Liveyre, Pey de l'Azé, Combe-Granal, and Badegoule. Some of these—as, for example, Les Eyzies and Le Moustier—are at a considerable height above the stream; but others—as La Madelaine and Laugerie—are little above the present flood-line; a proof that the level of the river is nearly the same as it was at the period during which these caves were inhabited.

The rivers of the Dordogne, says Sir John Lubbock,[*] run in deep valleys cut through calcareous strata; and while the sides of the valleys in chalk districts are generally sloping, in this case, owing probably to the hardness of the rock, they are very frequently vertical. Small caves and grottoes frequently occur; besides which, as the different strata possess unequal powers of resistance against atmospheric influences, the face of the rock is, as it were, hollowed out in many places, and thus "rockshelters" are produced. In very ancient times these were inhabited by men, as we know from the abundant evidences they have left of their presence. But, continues Sir John Lubbock, as civilization advanced, man, no longer content with the natural but inconvenient abode thus offered to him, excavated chambers for himself; and in some places the entire façade of the rock is honeycombed with doors and windows leading into suites of rooms, often in tiers one over another, so as to suggest the idea of a French Petra. In the stirring times of the Middle Ages we have no doubt they served as very effi-

* Sir J. Lubbock, "Pre-Historic Times," pp. 245-247.

cient fortifications, and even now some of them are still
in use as store-houses, and for other purposes.   At Brome-
tôme may be seen an old chapel cut in the solid rock,
resembling the rock-cut temples of Ellora and Elephanta.

Of the implements manufactured by the early inhabitants of these caves, and the bones of animals discovered
in conjunction with other relics, we shall not here speak.
It is certain, however, from the absence of metal, of
polished flint weapons, and of pottery—the evident ignorance of agriculture, and the apparent absence of all
domestic animals, including even the dog,—that they had
attained only a very low stage of civilization, and consequently belonged to a very remote period of antiquity.

GROTTO OF LONGARA.

The Grotto of Longara in Piedmont forms a single
chamber, whose roof is of moderate elevation, but which
is not less than 1300 feet in length.   Its breadth varies
from 10 to 320 feet.   At the entrance it is not more
than nine feet wide, and the obstruction offered by an
enormous rock prevents more than one person passing at
a time.   There is nothing specially remarkable in this
vast hall ; but it is for ever doomed to the abhorrence of
all generous and sympathizing hearts by the memory of
an atrocious crime which, in the space of a few minutes,
made upwards of two thousand victims.

In 1520 the French army, after a disastrous campaign
in Italy, had fought its way back to the frontier.   The
rear-guard, commanded by the Chevalier Bayard, having
halted at Longara, a number of the fierce adventurers
who then composed the strength of every army, profiting

by the disorder inseparable from a harassed retreat, spread themselves over the country, and plundered it frightfully. The principal inhabitants assembled a couple of thousand of the peasantry, and advised them to take refuge with their families and an abundant supply of provisions in the cavern we have described. But the adventurers, having forced some of the country people to point out this retreat, hastened thither, burning to secure the plunder. In vain the hapless fugitives attempted to soften the hearts of these executioners, and to implore mercy for their wives and children. Reduced to desperation, they barricaded the entrance as best they could, and, favoured by the natural strength of the grotto, repulsed the first bandits who presented themselves. The latter returned to the charge in great numbers, but could not force the entrance of the cavern. Exasperated by their defeat, they conceived the atrocious design of subduing the resistance of their victims in a more effectual manner. They collected an immense pile of hay, straw, and green wood, in front of the grotto, and set it on fire.* The smoke penetrated into the cave, which was without any outlet, and, a few moments afterwards, the two thousand unfortunate creatures shut up in it, the greater number of whom were women, children, and old men, perished in terrible agony.

Bayard, indignant at this act of barbarity, hunted down these cowardly but ferocious adventurers, and hung the two guiltiest opposite the mouth of the cavern. It is related that while these wretches were in the hands of the executioners, a spectre, horribly lank and meagre,

---

* This abominable stratagem was repeated by the French army during its campaign in Algeria, under Marshal Bugeaud.

not pale, but blackened by the smoke, was seen to drag himself out of the cavern, throwing around him glances of the wildest affright.   He was a youth of fourteen, and the only human being who had survived the catastrophe. Bayard gave orders that he should receive all the assistance which his condition required, and was unable to retain his tears while listening to the youth's lamentable story of the death of his companions.   The pen refuses to repeat the horrors which are recorded in the narratives of contemporary authors; their nature may be judged from a single incident.

Some gentlemen, at the moment that the smoke began to fill the cavern, desirous of a soldier's death, had attempted to force their way out, that they might die, at all events, sword in hand.   But the peasants fell upon them and disarmed them.   The approach of an inevitable death could not appease the traditional jealousies of the lower against the upper orders, and these miserable creatures were massacred in the darkness, when all, noble or serf, were on the point of perishing by a common fate. "No," said the peasants, "you will not escape from hence; you brought us here, and here you shall die with us."

"And you, my friend," said Bayard to the young man, "how is it that you escaped?"

"I perceived," he said, "a feeble ray of light in a corner of the grotto; there I placed my mouth, more by instinct than reflection.   I soon lost consciousness, and thought myself dead; but the little air which penetrated through the imperceptible cranny prevented me from being suffocated.   On recovering myself, I remembered all that had transpired, but I was alone.   It has taken me a long, long time to drag myself out of yonder fatal cavern."

"I will have the bodies of the victims buried in consecrated ground," said Bayard; "and you shall see the murderers hung!"

_____

GROTTO OF CAMÖENS, AT MACAO.

Among the grottoes rendered famous by their associa-

GROTTO OF CAMÖENS, AT MACAO.

tions with historic personages, we may mention that of Camoëns, at Macao, on the coast of China.

It is needless to remind the reader that the life of the author of the "Lusiad" was a series of adventures. After having served in several expeditions, directed by the viceroy of the Portuguese colonies in India, against the mercantile fleets of Egypt, Camoëns in October 1558 returned to Goa, where he found a governor whose administration was of the most vicious and shameful character. Incapable of disguising his thoughts, Camoëns by some sharp sarcasms, drew down upon his head the hatred of this vindictive and all-powerful personage, who seized the pretext of a satire entitled " Disparates na India" (Vagaries in India)—in which the soldier-poet however, had not attacked any individual, but simply inveighed against the general corruption of colonial manners—to exile him to Macao.

Scarcely had he arrived in this city—which is situated three thousand leagues from Lisbon, his birth-place, and at the extremity of the known world—than he received the sad tidings of the death of a wife whom he passionately loved. Abandoned to solitude, overcome with humiliation and injustice, deprived of everything which could console his grieving spirit, Camoëns forgot his misfortunes and his despair in his pursuit of the Muse. In the grotto which still bears his name, and to which no enlightened traveller fails to perform a pilgrimage, this unfortunate man of genius composed the greater part of his immortal epic. In 1560, however, he was recalled to Goa.

SALT-MINES OF WIELICZKA.

The immense excavations which the industry and avarice of man have formed in the bowels of the earth for the purpose of extracting their stores of mineral wealth, scarcely belong to our subject. Yet the singular the unique aspect of the salt-mines of Wieliczka, and their numerous caverns, which suggest the idea of a subterranean palace of gnomes and fairies, seem to justify us in attempting a concise description.

Wieliczka (pronounced *Vielitchka*) is a small town of four thousand inhabitants, situated eight miles south-east of the ancient city of Cracow, at the foot of the Carpathian or Krapack Mountains, in that part of Poland which an infamous partition handed over to Austria.

It is famous for its immense salt-mines, which are worked over an area of three miles in length from north to south, and three-quarters of a mile in width from east to west, at a depth of one thousand feet. We do not know precisely at what date the mines of Wieliczka were discovered; but we know that they were already being worked in the early years of the twelfth century. A popular legend, related by Adam Streller, explains their discovery in a quaintly original manner :—

The Princess Cunigunde of Hungary, the betrothed of Boleslaus the Chaste, king of Poland, was unwilling to accept any dowry from her father, either in gold or silver; but on her way into Poland she passed through the salt-mines of Hungary, and threw into them her nuptial ring. Having arrived at Cracow, Cunigunde halted there, ordered her attendants to lead her to Wieliczka, and directed them to excavate the earth in her presence. Her commands were obeyed, and a salt-mine of incomparable wealth was discovered. In the first block of salt extracted from it was found the princess's ring.

At the present day these mines employ no fewer than a thousand workmen, to say nothing of four hundred horses, and form an important contribution to the Austrian revenues. In 1850 their products were estimated at nine hundred and sixty two thousand quintals.

It has been calculated that to visit in detail the inter

SALT-MINES OF WIELICZKA.

minable labyrinths o galleries, halls, and magazines, which mul tiply under the visitor' steps, would occupy period of four weeks, a the rate of eight hours marching daily. The total length of the gal leries is computed a 265 miles.

One of the curiosities of these immense excavations which reflect on every side, like crystal, the shimmer o lamps and torches, is the Chapel of St. Antony, situate on the first tier or stage. This chapel is constructed in the mine itself, and composed of nothing but salt; altars statues, columns, ornaments,—all are of salt.

On the second tier lies a lake of 500 feet in length and 40 feet in depth, formed by the percolation of the moisture through the salt. Visitors are carried across this lake in a little boat. The flickering gleam of the torches in the midst of the deep shadows, the skiff silently gliding over the waters, the incessant strokes of the pick axe, the explosion of gunpowder charges to loosen the masses of salt, awake in the soul the idea of an infernal world, and impress it with a kind of religious terror.

The mines of Wieliczka have been several times the theatre of brilliant festivals, of which the most memor able took place on the occasion of the marriage of Queen

CHAPEL OF ST. ANTHONY   SALT-MINES OF WIELICZKA.

Sophia and Wladislas Jagillon, in 1624. Whenever a
sovereign or a member of the imperial family of Austria
visits these magnificent mines, they are decorated in

the most magnificent style, and splendidly illuminated;
lustres, mirrors, and draperies are arranged in a vast and
regular saloon; a circular gallery, supported by pillars
of salt, is set apart as an orchestra, whose harmonies
produce a marvellous effect under these resonant roofs.
The spectacle is one of which the liveliest imagination
can scarcely form an idea; and our poets in their most
extravagant visions have invented nothing to equal it.

THE CATACOMBS OF PARIS.

We have seen that in several districts of France the
existence has been definitively established of a great
number of subterranean habitations excavated in the
rocks long ages ago, and which have since been made use
of, sometimes as places of refuge during the prevalence of
civil strife, and sometimes as the retreat of brigands.
Now it is of no rare occurrence for travellers to mistake
these subterranean habitations for catacombs.   But not
the less do there occur in many parts of France crypts,
sepulchral chapels, and finally, genuine catacombs.

Upon these various underground cemeteries it will be
needless to dwell at length, but, among the most remarkable, we may cite the crypts of St. Germain d'Auxerre,
which are arranged in two stories; the crypt and catacombs of Saint Pothien, Bishop of Lyons, and those of St.
Irenaeus, his successor; the subterrenos of the Abbey of
St. Victor of Marseilles; the catacombs or crypts of St.
Trophimus and St. Honorat, at the foot of the hill of
Aliscamps (*Campus Elisius*), now the cemetery of the
Champs-Elysées at Arles; the catacombs of the Cordeliers
at Toulouse; the celebrated sepulchral chapels of St.

Denis, which enshrine the tombs of the French kings; those, finally, of the Church of St. Geneviève of Paris, known under the name of the Catacombs of the Pantheon, which have received the remains of many great men, and especially of Jean Jacques Rousseau and Voltaire.

As for what are improperly called the Catacombs of Paris, some words of explanation are desirable. The reader will err wofully if he believes that these subterranean galleries date from a remote antiquity, and are the primitive burial-places of the ancient inhabitants of Caesar's or Julian's *Lutetia*. Nor must he believe that, like the catacombs of Rome, or those of Egypt, they contain the bodies of the aboriginal population preserved by the embalmer's art, or reduced to skeletons but preserved intact. The catacombs of Paris are simply the quarries whence has sprung in great part the magnificent capital of France, and into which have been transported, within the last half-century, the bones of the ancient cemeteries formerly so common in Paris. Therefore they do not contain any body complete and intact, but an enormous quantity of bones of every kind, all mingled and confused together, with the exception of a certain number which have been collected and grouped together under the common designation of the cemetery whence they have been removed.

But here we enter upon some details which, we are not without hope, may prove interesting to the reader.

It is known that, up to the end of the reign of Louis XVI., the principal Parisian cemetery was the one called Cemetery of the Innocents, situated beside the church of that name. Anciently established beyond the circuit of

Paris, between the two suburbs of Old and New Saint-Germain, the Beau-Bourg and the Bourg-l'Abbé, near the gate north of the town which stands at the intersecting points of the two roads of Saint-Denis and Montmartre, it occupied a site known under the name of the *Campela* or the *Champeaux;* but the enlargement of Paris progressed so rapidly that soon this cemetery, or church, as it is often called, occupied the centre of the city. Philip Augustus, in 1186, surrounded it with high walls. At a later date, in 1218, it was enlarged by the addition of a piece of ground belonging to it, on the side of the *halles.*

The danger to the public health of this immense mass of putridity, where, for upwards of two centuries, so many generations had successively died out or been destroyed, was fully understood; and urgent petitions were frequently addressed to the French Parliament, imploring it to abate the nuisance. At length, in 1780, after some serious calamities had occurred, the lieutenant-general of police, M. Lenoir, received a petition, in which the injuries to the public health arising from such a hecatomb of slaughter were pointedly stated; the number of bodies interred, exceeding all measure and incapable of being counted, had raised the soil upwards of eighteen feet above the level of the neighbouring streets and houses: it was estimated that in the period between 1186 and 1758,—that is to say, in a period of six centuries only,—one million two hundred thousand bodies had been deposited in the cemetery, and it had never ceased to be used as the burial-place of upwards of twenty parishes, without counting the Hôtel Dieu and what was formerly called the Basse Geôle.

Finally, on the 9th of November 1785, a decree of

the Council of State, on the proposition of M. Lenoir, ordered the suppression of the cemetery of the Innocents, and its conversion into a public market.

The question then arose, To what site should the innumerable bones be removed which had formerly been accumulated in this cemetery? The ancient quarries, situated under the plain of Mont-Souris, at the place called the Tombe-Isoire or Isouard, seemed, from their proximity to the city, and also from their extent, to be very favourable for the establishment of the great subterranean cemetery.

But it was necessary, in the first place, to repair those vast quarries, which, having been abandoned for several centuries, had fallen in at many points, and been rendered very dangerous by landslips and pools of water. A whole twelvemonth of preliminary work placed their interminable tunnels in a condition to receive the bones exhumed from the cemetery of the Innocents, and those which might be successively removed from the other cemeteries, charnel-houses, and mortuary chapels of the city of Paris.

On the 7th of April 1787 took place the benediction and consecration of the enclosure of the catacombs of the Tombe-Isoire. On the very day of this ceremony, and immediately the consecration was ended, the transportation began of the bones of the cemetery of the Innocents to the new catacombs; an operation which lasted for fully fifteen months.

After the cemetery of the Innocents, those of St. Eustatius and St. Etienne des Grés were the next to furnish their contingent to the immense ossuary.

The bloody struggles of the Revolution occurring mean-

while, the mortal remains of the victims of August 28
and 29, 1788, of April 28, 1789, of August 10. 1792, and
of the 2nd and 3rd of September, in the same year, were
successively transported to the catacombs.   Certain special
inscriptions point out to the attention of the explorer the
bones of the unfortunate defenders of the *ancien régime.*

Since that dark epoch there have been removed into
the ossuary the bones exhumed from the old churches of
St. Landry, St. Julien des Ménétriers, St. Croix de la
Bretonnerie, des Bernardins, St. André des Arts or des
Arcs, St. Jean de l'Hôtel de Ville, otherwise called St.
Jean en Grève, of the Capucins St. Honoré, of the
Blancs Manteaux, of the Hospitallers of the Petit Saint
Antoine, of St. Nicolas des Champs, of the Holy Ghost,
of St. Lawrence, St. Benoît, all churches which, one after
the other, were demolished.

All these bones, as they were removed, were piled up
symmetrically along the galleries, of which they thus
formed to a certain extent the side walls.   The number
of corpses brought to this funereal receptacle has been
computed at three millions in all.

The decoration of this subterranean City of the Dead
is in harmony with its gloomy destination.   It consists of
a regular and symmetrical arrangement of the bones.
The apophyses of the great bones of the legs and arms are
brought forward in such a manner as to exhibit an almost
level surface, which, at intervals, is traversed by a row of
skulls, above which is placed another layer of great bones;
the severe monotony of these dreary walls being sometimes interrupted by a couple of tibias arranged in the
form of a cross.   Some of the crypts, or mortuary chambers, appropriated to the bones of a particular cemetery,

VIEW IN THE CATACOMBS OF PARIS.

are decorated with a fantastic coquetry; with garlands or wreaths of skulls, and tibias and cubitus intertwining as the more or less felicitous framework of the pyramids outlined on the background of the wall by another arrangement of skulls. These strange attempts at embellishment do not add to the serious reflections which the spectacle is so well calculated to awaken in the mind of every thoughtful visitor.

To the curious who descend into the catacombs is generally shown a small spring which was discovered during the filling up of the catacombs, and around which a little basin has been constructed. To this has been given the name of the Fountain of the Samaritan Woman; suggested by the inscription engraved upon it, which embodies the words of our Saviour to the Samaritan woman, whom He met at Jacob's Well, near Sychar, and whom He reminded of all things that ever she had done. In the month of November 1813, four red fish, gilded cyprini or Chinese dorados, were deposited in the basin, where they became perfectly acclimatized; but they disappeared long ago, and no successors have been found to them.

The so-called "Tomb of Gilbert" is simply a consolidation, in the form of a sepulchral monument, raised at a point where signs of decay became visible. It has received the name of the unfortunate poet from the well-known lines in his poem of the "Last Judgment," which have been engraved upon it :—

> " Au banquet de la vie, infortuné convive,
>   J'apparus un jour, et je meurs ;
>   Je meurs, et, sur la tombe, où lentement j'arrive,
>   Nul ne viendra verser des pleurs."

[One day, an unfortunate guest, I sit at the banquet of life; I die, and on the tomb which I slowly reach no one drops a tear.]

A decorative form has been given likewise in several other places to the buttresses necessary for the safety of the works. Thus, we meet with the Pillar of Remembrance, which is triangular; the great Sacellum of the Obelisks; the Pillar of the Imitation, which is square; the triangular Obelisk; the Sepulchral Lamp; the Pedestal of St. Lawrence; the Great Pillar of the Clementine Nights.

The ventilation of the catacombs is provided for by means of shafts carried into the cellars of the houses situated above them; they are opened only at necessary intervals.

As for the shafts or staircases by which we descend into the catacombs, they are sixty-three in number. Some are inside, and some are outside the city. They are most numerous in the faubourgs Saint Marcel, Saint Jacques, and Saint Germain, as well as at Chaillot: there is also a certain number outside Paris, from south to west, and from east to south. These entrances, however, are reserved for the workmen and officials charged with the supervision and reparation of the catacombs. Visitors are admitted by a staircase constructed at the barrier of the Maine, in the court of the ancient octroi. This snail-like staircase, which numbers not fewer than ninety steps, abuts on a very narrow but well kept gallery, leading, with many turns and windings, into the ossuary: the visitor returns by another and similar gallery, terminating at a second staircase of seventy-eight steps. These galleries bear, in characters strongly incrusted in the wall, the names of the streets of Paris, whose direction they follow underground, so that it is impossible for any accident to occur.

Very few words are necessary as to the inscriptions which were engraved, shortly after the inauguration of the catacombs, and also at later dates, at the entrance or in the principal passages. These inscriptions, of which the best and the best chosen are borrowed from the Prophets or from the *Imitatio Christi*, are frequently selected from poets who were formerly popular, as Lemercier, Legouvé, Lemoine, Ducis, De-lille; and a few are taken from Malfilâtre, Gilbert, and Lamartine.

A register was formerly kept, in which visitors were permitted to record in verse and prose the thoughts suggested by an inspection of the catacombs. We do not know whether it still exists; but if it has disappeared we should not regret it, for its pages were loaded with the dreariest and most exaggerated commonplaces. The following extracts are the only two which exhibited any merit :—

> " Je suis grand partisan de l'ordre,
> Mais je n'aime pas celui-ci.
> Il peint un éternel désordre,
> Et, quand il vous consigne ici,
> Dieu jamais n'en révoque l'ordre."
>
> COUSSON.

[That is : I am a great partizan of order, but I do not care for this. It paints an eternal disorder, and when He consigns you here, God never revokes the order.]

> " Nous naissons pour mourir un jour :
> Cet arrêt n'excepte personne.
> Peut-être est-ce aujourd'hui mon tour ;
> Mais à mon sort je m'abandonne.
> Aveugle et stupide troupeau,
> Que la mort chasse devant elle,
> Nous passons du trône au tombeau,
> Du jour à la nuit éternelle.
> Mais non, l'homme ne s'endort pas,
> Pour ne plus revoir la lumière.
> Au jour marqué pour le trépas,
> Il commence une autre carrière ;

> Il retrouve un père, un ami,
> Dans une demeure immortelle ;
> Et j'y reverrai Noémi,
> Pour ne plus me séparer d'elle."
>
> L. MICHAUD.

[We are born to die ; none are excepted from this law. Perhaps it is my turn to-day ; but I abandon myself to my fate. The blind and silly herd which Death drives before him, we pass from the throne to the tomb, from the day to eternal night. But no : man does not sleep, never again to behold the light. On the day pre-ordained for his departure he commences another career ; he finds again a father, a friend, in an immortal habitation ; and I shall once more see Noémi, never again to be separated from her.]

Is not a grave and reverent silence the best homage which we can pay to these memorials of generations gone before us ; and does it not seem useless, at all events, to endeavour by little literary effusions to mitigate the gloominess of a spectacle which has a philosophical teaching of its own ?

www.ingramcontent.com/pod-product-compliance
Lightning Source LLC
Chambersburg PA
CBHW020621030726
47497CB00007B/2353